G

Glasgow

Edited by
Ruthie Kennedy,
Colin Herd & Tommy Pearson

Dostoyevsky Wannabe Cities
An Imprint of Dostoyevsky Wannabe

First Published in 2021
by Dostoyevsky Wannabe Cities
All rights reserved
© All copyright reverts to individual authors

Dostoyevsky Wannabe Cities is an imprint of
Dostoyevsky Wannabe publishing.

www.dostoyevskywannabe.com

This book is a work of fiction. The names, characters and incidents
portrayed in it are the work of the authors' imagination. Any resemblance
to actual persons, living or dead, events or localities is entirely coincidental.

Cover design by Dostoyevsky Wannabe Design
Interior Design by Tommy Pearson, Pomegranateditorial

ISBN: 9798423762728

No parts of this publication may be reproduced, stored in a retrieval
system, or transmitted in any form or by any means, electronic,
mechanical, photocopying, recording, or otherwise, without the prior
written permission of the copyright owner.

Contents

Foreword

In 2019, when we accepted the offer to edit this anthology, the world looked different. For a start, we had 'real life' meetings in a 'real life' office and we spoke with certainty about events as if they were really going to happen. Looking back, what a thrill it was to be in the company of another living person! Writing now, in 2021, each rare time I'm in the presence of more than one other person I don't live with, I feel this thrill in my body that I never noticed before. I can only assume that it has always been there, part of the secret pleasure of living as a social creature. It's almost exciting to live in this inbetween moment, this weird space 'between' lockdowns, where I can just about hold simultaneously in my mind the numbness of permanent isolation and the electric promise of sociality. When things go 'back to normal', I won't notice the excitement any more. Which is as it should be! But I'm thankful all the same for this little peek behind the curtain.

Many of the pieces in this anthology occupy this same in-between space: collaborations devised in isolation, inhabiting a 'Glasgow of the mind'. Even before the pandemic, this was a hope that we held for the anthology. To our minds, collaboration is at the heart of what makes Glasgow unique - as the signs say, People Make Glasgow. And we tried to be as broad as we could when considering who 'counts' as a Glaswegian poet, asking for submissions from anyone who felt they had a connection with the city. So this idea of collaboration across space was already baked into the anthology. Then the pandemic made it essential.

Having been created during what is undoubtedly the most disruptive global health crisis in our lifetimes, this anthology is as much a time capsule as it is a place capsule. Rowan Bland, Siam Hatzaw, Alice Hill-Woods, Asta Kinch and Scott Norval's collection of pieces are linked by the views from their respective windows over lockdown, while Georgi Gill and Gillian Shirreffs' perfectly titled 'singular together' is equally raw and comforting, providing visceral accounts of Lockdown 1.0 which are still infused with a sly and knowing humour.

Other collaborations, such as Eilidh and Fionn Duffy's 'I Think the Plants in My Phone Are Trying to Tell Me Something' and Jim Colquhoun & Jamie McNeill's 'Of Thirlage And Suckeners' look outwards to nature rather than the claustrophobia of staying at home.

Some pieces veer into dreams and surreality such as Maria Sledmere and Kirsty Dunlop's 'a little kilo of dreams' and Denise Bonetti and Jamie Bollard's 'Another Zombie Nerfland'.

Still more pieces turn a more critical eye to their approach, such as Gaar Adam's and EC Lewis's "The New Pantheon", and "Skirts" by Esther Draycott, Gwen Dupré and Kiah Endelman Music.

And of course, you will notice throughout the anthology that each collaboration is utterly unique, whether they are about Glasgow or of Glasgow. We couldn't be prouder to present to you this anthology, which absolutely deserves to be read time and again, and which we hope will continue to provide a hint about what makes Glaswegian writing Glaswegian for years to come.

Phew. This book! What the hell is it?! In a post on his journal in 2013, Tom Leonard, whose influence is everywhere here, wrote:

"Not just to change the nature of the debate, but to change the nature of the space it inhabits. Absolutely not to accept the contours of the space provided. Some will understand the meaning in politics. Harder, much harder, to understand the meaning in writing."

This book - which has been so brilliantly supported by the visionary publishers Dostoyevsky Wannabe - stretches, expands and doesn't "accept the contours of the space provided". Literally, because it is more voluminous than we could have anticipated. More conceptually too, because each collaboration in here messes with, and counters, the contours of the space provided: by the city, by writing, by the idea of authorship.

I always find it a little tempting to read poems as a verb in the title of Leonard's 1967 *Six Glasgow Poems*, even if the quantity prefix makes that awkward. Poem-ing feels like something that Glasgow (like everywhere else) does, something that, as one of the poems nearly puts it, wirraw in thigithir. This anthology celebrates poem-ing together: being awake to language as social in all its thrills, in all its misuses too.

It's a privilege to have worked on a Glasgow edition of the

Cities anthology series. We thought quite a bit about what it means to celebrate / anthologise the writing of / around / in a city? And one reason why it seems important can be summed up in a beautiful Prayer poem by Langston Hughes to all the inhabitants of "our weary city". Living together in large conurbations is wearying. Hughes though, was a radical poet of collective agency, and I can't help but see a kind of blueprint in his choice of "weary" for the transformation that the collaborative poetics here perform, turning "weariness" to "we are-y ness": a creative social and poetic force.

In my dreams, I've bumped into everybody in this book numerous times although we haven't really met. In these dreams we talk about the tender adjacencies in Glasgow's density and vastness that re-frame and mirror our re-inhabiting of familiar spaces; we talk about the book as a virtual home that has sustained itself through an erotics of glimpses— shimmering skin and text and image— across the seasons of its production. We talk about the joy in carrying collaboration around with us like the cuddliest, most confrontational soft toy. It's been, in waking, a pleasure to edit this anthology in a time in which we couldn't touch or meet, and especially so when the contributions on display here engage the abundance of Glasgow's experiments with form, with intimacy and, above all, with the reflective and generous strengths of collaboration.

Ruthie, Colin & Tommy

Rowan Bland
Siam Hatzaw
Alice Hill-Woods
Asta Kinch
Scott Norval

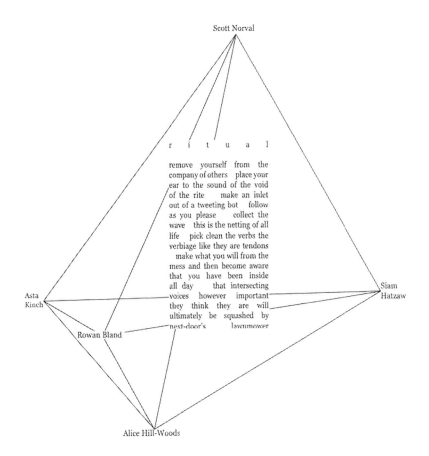

Scott Norval

r i t u a l

remove yourself from the
company of others   place your
ear to the sound of the void
of the rite   make an inlet
out of a tweeting bot   follow
as you please   collect the
wave   this is the netting of all
life   pick clean the verbs the
verbiage like they are tendons
  make what you will from the
mess and then become aware
that you have been inside
all day   that intersecting
voices   however   important
they think they are will
ultimately be squashed by
next-door's   lawnmower

Asta
Kinch

Rowan Bland

Siam
Hatzaw

Alice Hill-Woods

17

there is
nothin worse
than when
people act
all fake and

---

there's a 4
pack of wild
berry rekorderlig at
your
doorstep
listen cunt
i knew you
were a snake

---

my biology
teacher
made me sit
out of the

class
because she knew i was a lesbian
this "roses are red" patter isn't funny
any more.

furloughed flights at glasgow airport — i am
                    deeply deeply
                    sorry but
                    thumb rings make
                    me feel so secure
really sad that insta stories weren't about during
                    the T in the park era
                    what a horrible cunt of a woman
                    she 'wanted boris to die'
                    vile

today i was gifted a rainbow
and a sycamore and a hawthorne
in dennistoun park.

                    who knew lockdown
            would give me self
confidence
                    do you know how rude
                            it is to walk
                    through a secured park
            and not close the gate?

                                        ...

glad the trains
are really quiet—
we got more lovely flowers today from   friends
because of our cancelled wedding
not sure that's a
good thing.

join the fight

and end with

what the
fuck?

Rowan

Day 1

You're full of anemones today, and what next?
A love like calling tinned peaches to ripen.
All this roses are red isn't funny anymore.

So cheers to you—
to win is sympathy, failing miserably.

When did my needs feel catered for?

Just as well,
you didn't want to deliver all we shared.
I am deeply, deeply sorry.

Not sure that's a good thing.

All this to say, you deserted my grief
which is to say, you deserved gold
(all I see is rain on stories on stories)
    what a gutter.

Day 2

AUCTION:

Don't want any risks, ok? Madness is doing a valuable job as it is. We started as a poem, failed as a poem. Hey. There's someone in your life who needs to know you love them. Here we go. Today I was gifted: a rainbow, anemones, a cancelled wedding. Today can absorb the road when it wants to. Real responses only.

Day 3

Here... here
such a sense.

Today is Saturday and on Saturdays
we danced.

> *I don't want to fight.*
> *Someone tell me when I'm*

listening.

Day 4

Thank you, Winter,
been watching with love.
Of ordinary life, the heart warms.

Strangers calling
told me to change.

Day 5

The smile on your face again, I'm wearing it like a dress. And I know it was tasteless but staying is not easy. Can you hear me? This self, where no one seems to be? As long as I am breathing, I will always worship you. I know it seems unlikely. Like I was created for a book.

Day 6

Turning off as
the end is near.

I love
as much as the next.

Operating loss with higher
costs when—
hope is found.

Double back,
Spirit calls,
brings me outside, says:

Look what's appeared

a little oak, just there
all set to grow.

And it was good.

This, my liturgy:

Rain lands on

one windowpane
and not another.

25

Day 7

A round of applause. The only thing that kept me sane was you giving me your all while I'm away. Who am I to deny it? I was an emergency. A monster you slept under. *Who remembers the streets dancing?* Another little peace. I was always hoping for a better run, the day I want so badly. Another lost. And all this pure to share until—what's left? In the midst, it's important to remember it's a game.

Were you there? Where's your memory?

To hope in you was a change.
Slowly, slowly, and all too drastic.

Siam

simmer town

a body makes a turn for the junction
flummoxed lights signal l/r
their swarmish clicks silenced
by hardbutsoft interiors

        tinned peach curdle of a sky

if i had to give you a clue i would
hide it in the ferny clyde intestine
that runs from one here to another

        the clue would be wet
        gossamer
            pushed
        from its snuggery

you would have to pry the slick stone
slough off the ordinary life
from the soapberry
        to make out my noise
which is me saying that
i am finely tuned to your motives

i would rather not commission
an answer

yet all around
the ospreys make their plainchant known

thank you gutter. i will be wintering in love.

Alice

aching   without limbs   Praying for
morningsong
with the   limbs now   in plain
stillness   licking   woodensong
pews
the stillness of   licking
spilled   the bed raw   there was never
couscous   with conscious   a head without
hours
with
in-between
with

representing   with   Flummoxed
what was   slicing   mews prey with
never   breast to
an answer   hip   unconscious
but a dictum   bone

slab-stone
I shall   with a
cheese knife
I shall be sure   reproducing

these cells
barely
like   a body   I shall be sure
for midnight   to be there

gossamer

      for midnight   I shall

gossamer   pays   commission
heads
falling   in breaking   midnight
    news of
gossamer
lavender   lightness

        Gossamer
        dreams

        within and
        without

    stones clicking stones licking
    scriptless   weightless

reaking   in B   stones ticking
from the   clockless
ritual

and   telephone   With a story
worming   whispers   a story
eats
    a snake   with a wave

and knowledge for the time
eats
                        watching
           a snake   the watching
if I were for the duration
a worm   and asking in
asking   whispers

I'd simply a snake

worm myself
wooden

secreting   and   Like a tree
messages   this
                        to Eden
all   is my
curtains go nothing   very
the masking ritual   there
way   in sleep
            all curtains
all curtains   in sleep
            I go to sleep I go to sleep
open   all curtains

                        This Monday
copying and pasting from tubes This Monday
opening

                                        Asta

looking out the window over the years   breaking
from the ritual of our everyday lives
          trying to say   nobody is listening
nobody is doing anything   I AM ANGRY

we are just watching from our windows
our eyes blink dryly at bright blue late night light
and in the morning   when we rise
we pick up tongues   from different
dimensions

the spoken word reopens our endings
underneath we find two different ways of being
of saying   what is this???? the randomness
of needing an ending

people share the stars   to create an ending is
to send something forward
                    in the randomness of our need
the spoken news of the people   is trying
                              has said

this is dying boldly   this is watched footage
          JOIN THE FIGHT

so we share   we deliver the growth
on the tube   our lives   help the fighting the rush

reeds of wholesale slaughter
          fighting   this watched footage what is the right
course   mourning morning
          off work till july

          news to the people ending with
                                   what the fuck

                              Scott

Fionn Duffy
Eilidh Duffy

I Think the Plants in My Phone Are Trying to Tell Me Something

There is an emotion which stirs me from time to time. It is a short-lived feeling of arriving, only to realise there is more to come. Apparently there is no word for it in the English language so I've decided to call it arrepture. An etymological love-child of arrival and departure, it is what surfaces when we reach a point that has been within our sights but realise we must go further. It's not quite disappointment, not quite acceptance, but something that sits tremulously between them.

It speaks close to rupture, a word I like for its soft u's, globular consonants and common use to describe a fleshy tear. And sounds similar to rapture, a feeling of bliss, or – if you're a specific type of Christian – the event that brings about humanity's ascendance to heaven and the end of time.

Arrepture manifests differently depending on each subject and their immediate context. Like reading a novel or watching a film, the mental and physical space we occupy defines our relationship to the experience. Knowing that there is more to come, a mysterious and unfamiliar more, can be magical. Not-knowing can instil hope and desire. But it can also bring on an uneasy weight – the kind that sits at the back of your head where neck meets skull.

My earliest recollections of arrepture are moments I recognise from childhood walks up Conic Hill. (You remember, right?) It is situated just outside of Glasgow on the banks of Loch Lomond. We called it dragon hill, named for its humps which rise and fall like the back of a reclining monster.

References to dragon lore in the area don't seem to exist but we have always personified hills, giving them characters, stories and souls. There are numerous words to describe hills in Gaelic, all referencing a different form and location. Often they are named after human anatomical features.

There's one in particular I'm thinking of which surprised me not so long ago – it's soft, round curvature faithfully resembles a breast with the cairn on top

a perfect nipple.

There's a Flat Earther Society in Inverness. They give you coffee if you sit and talk to them about their theories for a while. It's very nice in there, all pinewood panelling. If it wasn't for the conspiratorial posters and banners you would think it was a coffee shop in Shoreditch (sans neons, perhaps). The last time I visited I met a man who is convinced the world is flat and in the shape of a beautiful woman's body (lying down of course, I'm not sure he had a theory for what happened to her back).

> And when I noticed that busty hill for a moment I thought I might believe him.

Landscapes are often turned by the imagination into feminine shapes (mother nature, amirite?). From the Calanais Standing Stones on the Isle of Lewis you can see over to 'na Mòinteach, the Old Woman of the Moors, a mountain far in the distance which resembles the profile of a sleeping woman.

And then there is, of course, The Cailleach. Divine hag.

> You sent us a video, not far back, of you placing a handful of snow on a low stone dyke. Rather than a divisional feature, the dyke is the wall of a house. The house of The Cailleach. You had told me about this place before. It is where The Cailleach and her family stay, small stone figures, in a glen that takes a while to walk in to, some place around the midriff of the country.

> She lives in many places, and has lent her name to sites scattered through Scotland, Ireland and the islands between. She turns the water at Corryvreckan and gives her form to the hills of Skye. Her face is carved by the elements into the cliffs at Moher where

she looks out woefully across the Atlantic. Even in the concrete bowels of Glasgow there remains an area named Haghill.

She is the queen of winter, a creator, the weather and our ancestors. She throws her cloak of frost across the landscape and uses her hammer to drum up storms and winds. Today is February 1st, the day on which she turns into Brigid, shedding her age and becoming a young woman once again. In Gaelic her name is pronounced breej-eh: sounding a breath pushed from the back of the throat and over the tongue.

You told me Cailleach, Bodach and their daughters live in a house. That they are brought into the sun at the turn of spring and put back inside as winter approaches. I don't know who does this every year. I can only guess they continue to care for the stones as a way to touch something that seems very rare, a piece of other-time. Of course it could also be that truly, without going through the motions, the glen would wither and die just as the story goes. But it would be a great risk to test the myth, and The Cailleach is not one to toy with.

Conic Hill comes from coinneach, which means moss. So it is a mossy hill, or was when it was named. It looks soft and green from the loch and sits neatly on the Highland Boundary Fault, a geological line which is acknowledged as the border between Highlands and Lowlands. If you look at a satellite image of Scotland, it's easy to trace a line diagonally between Stonehaven and Greenock, following the border between soft light green lowlands and the darker, muddier tones of the hills to the north.

All of these:
Moss Covered Rocks.

To climb this one we start in the Lowlands from the car park in Balmaha. The route through pine forest follows a dense path of brown needles that softly urge us up a steep and winding incline. Our first threshold is indicated by the light that peeks through thinner trees, the sky beyond the gate and sty at the edge of the wood.

As an adolescent this is the point where phone service would become patchy. I'm sure that these days it covers even the summit. (I wonder if they will ever build a brittle cellular tower up here like they have on some other, less popular hills.) In the early noughties these forced absences from the socio-political drama of high school infused every weekend venture out of Glasgow with a creeping sense of unrest.

These memories visit me for the first time in about a decade. I let them float down on to the top of my head and rest peacefully there. It's all green and smells sweet like sweat and earth, a dose of fresh air on human skin. Earth smells the way it does because of the bacteria that's in it. There is one in particular called Mycobacterium vaccae and it encourages serotonin production in the brain. It makes you happy.

I think the plants in my phone have been trying to tell me something. There is a chasm which runs down my middle, a split I try to put my finger on by writing.

When the blue glare of the screen throws green on to my retinas, I touch it: that valley, the glen.

> There is a question that has stumped theologians for years, the question of a metaphor in medieval hymns. Hildegard von Bingen used viriditas, "green-ness", as a word in place of god. It frustrates academics that she used the word so profusely.
> freshness,
> vitality,
> fertility,
> fecundity,
> fruitfulness,
> verdure,
> growth
> and the divine.

Makes sense, no?

I am on the plateau again, having
gone round it like a dog in circles
to see if it is a good place...I think
it is, and I am to stay up here for
a while.[1]

There's this meme that's been doing the rounds on Instagram. I don't know if you've seen it but basically it's a picture of a moss covered rock. I struggle now, to remember any other details.

Perhaps they don't matter.

No, the details don't matter. They don't matter because it was this image of a moss-covered-rock which appeared on the screen of my iPhone that made me realise that I really, truly wanted to be a moss-covered-rock. Craved it. I could feel its exterior, a damp, cold membrane (my own?) and its

They are sitting on a rock that is covered in moss. The body is holding a knife and wearing Doc Martens with flowers on the sides and they are whittling a 3d model of a pulsating blob GIF out of dead wood. It has too

45

gritty insides. Just for a
moment.

*many dimensions
and so they are
struggling to get
it right.[2]*

What a lovely fleeting
feeling it was.

Now that I think about it, I don't want to be the moss-covered-rock, I want to consume it. I want to lie draped across and feel a soft bounce give way to hard cold stone as I move my hands over its surface. I want its feathery moist bristles on my forearms, my shins, my face. I want that sequence of melting into and holding separate and feeling it all.

*It's the first thing
that I can remember.
Standing at the back
Window, looking at
the lawn, and
knowing exactly
everything beneath
it and wanting to get
back there. You don't
know how passionate
it is down there.[3]*

Now, I know what you
would say about this
mum.

"How morbid."

But the ground is fundamental.

(synonyms for fundamental
include root and elemental.)

It's all chemical, all passionate. You
know that.

In the little patch of garden outside our tenement the gravel comes in various shades of quartz. They are bright white, yellow, pink and red. I hold a fragment on my palm.
The little stone looks like a slice of red meat. I want to put it in my mouth.

It is the iron that gives it its hue, the same iron that gives red to our blood. Quartz is made from Silicon and Oxygen atoms. Silica and Oxygen are in our blood too. It stretches my brain to think of the processes which, by chance, caused those particles to form in this arrangement rather than that.

Gnarled roots – I've been dreaming of tangled plants throbbing with electricity – a knotted lump lying in a small space at my core they've latched themselves to my stomach lining and refuse to let go but I tug at them anyway I grab their twists and they spark like a disturbed network of underground cables I know if I prise them open I'll find muscle and sinew so I choose not to I don't want to see inside. I'm not ready for the stain on my hippocampus.
It's common knowledge that plants cause stains.

Bright green grass stains terrorise nice clean ladies
in adverts for laundry detergent.
Beetroot makes pink, onion skins yellow. The dyes for tweed
were made by pissing on lichen and letting it stew, then beat-
ing it hard with ammonia hands. Women's work of course.

On Conic Hill the path gets rocky, trees fall away
to brush and heather, then the land widens out and
curves around to the other side – the Highland side –
before we even start for the first summit. You would
sip coffee at this midway point, slowly. We would
sit on a wide flat rock and eat cheese sandwiches
and wait for you to finish at the place I often hoped
would be the end. My conviction as a sulky youth was
that these rituals were drawn out purely at my own
expense, lengthening my absence from everything
that really mattered – boys, bands, bebo.

There is an Irish word which can be used to define
the affinity one has with the landscape of their youth:
Dúchas, something the poet Seamus Heaney
describes as

connection, affinity or attachment [*to a place*] *due to descent or
long-standing; inherited, instinctual or natural
tendency.*[4]

I forget where I learned this, it seems relevant though.

I like Heaney, we share a fascination with peat bogs, and the marvellous powers of the moss to preserve any object that finds itself swallowed by sphagnum. Lost clothing, butter, kings and queens:

through my fabrics and skins
the seeps of winter
digested me,
the illiterate roots

pondered and died
in the cavings
of stomach and socket.
I lay waiting

on the gravel bottom,
my brain darkening,
a jar of spawn
fermenting under
ground [5]

I talked with this boy about death the other day. (Could have been yesterday, could have been last week time moves without regard for reason or rational charts these days.) Another person had just died as the virus, leering, danced closer into our personal sphere. For

this boy I talked with, when a person
dies a light switches off, there is a
total and abrupt
disintegration of something.

The End.

Moments like this fill me with a good dose of arrepture. Moments where I have assumed ("assumption
makes an ass of u and me", my boss once said) that
others perceive the world in the same way as I do. I
am catapulted into another being's perception and
desperately attempt to adopt it. I try his idea on like
a heavy woollen coat, but it's too wide in the shoulders, too short on my arms.

You see, I disagree with the boy. He hadn't
considered that we are vessels. We exist in relation
to one another, all glass and mirror reflecting
infinitely, the image altering as we move. Everything
that leaves us is just a chewed up version of some
other matter, each conversation built of symbols and
shapes requires a vessel to make it valid. (If a tree
falls in a forest does it make a sound etc. etc.) These
reflective surfaces leave bright burns on one another.
Like the stain of an object on the skin of a cyanotype,
it may not be a true replica of the other, but a faithful

interpretation subject to change.

Glasgow sits in a dip in the land. From my flat I can walk five minutes through Queens Park and see the Cathkin Braes. A long while ago men assembled on top of one of the hills where wind turbines now stand, to campaign for fair wages and universal suffrage.

Those men were weavers, they spent their time at looms at home, forming lengths of cotton cloth from the colonies. Those men were poets and they were gardeners, known for their care for flowers and intellectual gatherings. The government at the time was sanctioning economic austerity in response to the war in France and the weavers saw their breakfast turn from ham to porridge.

> Soup kitchens were stormed by those who were outraged that the authorities would make them line up or die of hunger, when each had been perfectly capable of providing for their families when wages had been fair. Two hundred years later I vote at a school around the corner. But now our food banks are used more frequently than ever before. Those merchants with power and friends in government continue to make and break laws as they please.

> *You always told me it takes time. It has taken my father's time, my mother's time. My uncle's time. My brother's*

and sister's time. My niece's and my nephew's time.
How much time do you want for your... 'progress'?[6]

Walk two minutes in the opposite direction and I can look out
to the Campsies at the end of Victoria Road.
                If I had the eyes of a mantis   shrimp and
turned my gaze slightly to the right I could see   the
site of the weaver's   sentencing, Tollcross.
Between   here and there.

The space between you and me is wide and who knows how
long it will remain so. But I find it funny, now, to think of the
monument we walked past day after day down in Nunhead
without realising the Scots it memorialises are those same
people punished for meeting here in Glasgow all those years
ago. Five sides, five men, five martyrs and almost 500 miles
from their home.

Distance collapses once we listen to the objects
in front of us.

Running round the memory again. Sweet and
        green and rose-tinted.

I can see beyond the city, but I cannot access it. I carry around
those hills at the edge of my vision when I buy groceries, or
pick up a prescription from Boots.

Now I've started dreaming about wires. (Sometimes I get sleep paralysis, you see, so dreams can have this funny effect on me that feels like memory.) Anyway, I dreamt my iPhone cable was burning. Woke up to a putrid plastic smell and looked at the cable as it spat out an orange glow. My memory of the faulty cable dimmed as the day began, but I felt a pinch of electricity when I tugged the charger out of its socket. I feel a pang realising the plants have gone, replaced with burning rubber.

But the mosses and lichen cling,
 breathing, and rub up against my
bones. The bacteria that make up
my micro-biome have emigrated
from those places I have been before,
and made their home in the creases
 of my skin and the depths of my
 gut. Isotopes, borne of the soil
 where my food was grown
(Kenya? Spain? Guatemala?) are
 lodged in   my bones,
                  my hair,
                  my nails.

The Science says I am a living, breathing map of all the worlds that I've consumed.

I already am/ate the moss and the rock.
It's inside me, seared in to memory.

Skin reeks of blue light.

Notes

1. From Nan Shepherd's *The Living Mountain*

2. Linda Stupart says it so eloquently in *Virus*

3. Reminds me of a passage from Claire-Louise Bennett's *Pond*

4. This quote is actually by Irish critic Brendan Devlin, but Heaney used it to explain his use of Dúchas in an essay about his translations of Sophocles Antigone

5. From *Bog Queen* by Seamus Heaney

6. James Baldwin speaks in the 1989 American Master documentary, "James Baldwin: The Price of the Ticket." Although he is referring to race, his highlighting of the distracting and destructive concept of linear human progress (as if racism, sexism, homophobia, transphobia, class etc. are all naturally occurring parts of humanity and not social constructs perpetuated by capitalism) can be applied here.

Shehzar Doja
Juana Adcock

IN A WAY

I

India Building by 1876

Building is a reed
    out of place
conjoined,
  weeded out — the sun
now never stops
to settle
      on its empirical
      rust — a root glimpses out,
stretches its arms towards the
perfection of another coral chippy.

There are 27 windows—barricaded,
glassed,
some splintered— all halo.
   Gift from the wards of a
     new world and freshly tinted
      grin

A man I know
  says he will buy this place.
      Walk me through these axial slit
      passageways, re—
        leasing silver coated spoons
A new body wakes
  and walks by—

IN A WAY THE CLYDE IS

But how, if we live enclosed by stone
In a dark and treeless valley of walls?
– Cesário Verde

a strip mine. Useful lifespan approximately 150 years. The value all extracted now. Yet the dredged silt's still hanging heavy over the ghost town left around it. Which lights up each night like an amusement park for no one. For spirits wandering in a Miyazaki film.

fordable. At low tide the depth is less than the span of my shoulders. On my feet at high tide and the surface licks just below my breasts. Yon ocht inches – eight islands – where trees and villagers live. Roll up your skirts and push out a wee paddle boat.

a razed temple. An earlier belief system and way of life destroyed to make way for the new doctrine. Clerics, giving up their poverty vows, approve of exploitation for profit. The land is hollowed to fill a power vacuum created by distant legal transferences.

a map of 1759. Men had barely learned how to draw straight lines on paper and already. Determined to "cleanse, scour,

straighten and improve" a defenceless natural shape. Joy
removed. Entanglements cut. Witches executed. In the name
of progress, and maps.

affordable. Child's play. A mathematical solution in a two-di-
mensional world. Flatland, before Edwin Abbott Abbott had
written his novella about a world built by squares. Cyclical
time deemed unscientific, and hammered out to resemble a
canal for the transit of goods.

fake news. A daemonologie written to glorify an orphaned
manchild who strives for power in lieu of – boring but true –
the love he never received. Panic-induced populace. Thirsty
for sensation. The devil may even be you. Stay vigilant. Destroy
all that is sensuous.

an investment plan. Where the sum of ecological resources
was squandered at the beginning and now nothing lives.
Where seagulls scan dronelike for chip trails on the drunken
paths of would-be sailors. Thriving in the chemical waste that
sixty years on still seeps.

a simulation of the Clyde. The Clyde imagining all the things
the Clyde could be if the Clyde were not the Clyde. Or if only
the Clyde were located in a more geographically advantageous
position. Such as a place where existing trade routes converge,
or anywhere south.

an abandoned factory. Its scale too vast for human comprehension, with no longer any conceivable use. Happily, illegally, we run free. We swim, sail, hold races. Lots of all-night parties. Barriers are knocked down. Padlocks broken. Bolt cutters in hand.

ripe for reclamation. For who owns this hindering of transit through our own home, these useless docking bays? Soon vegetation softening the bricks, heated pools, laughter, music, wildlife, fishing, floating markets, street food, whatever the weather. Unticketed.

overflowing. Flooding our living rooms. Forcibly made to carry, it comes in with a vengeance. Our bodies have been absorbing the excess damp, scarcity thinking all the while. Now we are the ones needing dredged. All we can do is pray to the Clyde. It says: play.

its own arisings. Volcanic rock blasted and disposed of at the edges. Energy made sluggish. Despite constant rain the sensation around it is always bone-dry. Mudcakes cooked in the sun in Haiti. The mud is mixed with salt, margarine and water. Good to eat.

a plantation. Species removed to make way for the monocrop. Indigenous peoples enslaved and dressed in tartan. The Highland Clearances, only done first in the Caribbean. An African queen caged, nominally free.
Still grappling with
the police brutality.

plastic money. Poured in from abroad. Growing forests of glitzy glass and steel buildings. An imitation of an imitation of luxury. The rot botchedly painted over. To appear sleek in brochures. Ignoring, then commodifying, the value generated by us who live here.

a theologian. With his head in the clouds, bent over written words, he crawls under the edge of the sky. He tells us he has found the place where heaven and earth meet. (It costs money.) His disregard for the realities of everyday life and chil-drearing,
a seeking for Truth.
a mirror. Needing no words or metaphors or comparisons. Patiently waiting each day. Yet rarely fully seen. Blinded by its own past, it shies away from its own reflection. Emotions denied, it snags on sentimental narrative, repeats tired phrases to hide away grief.

a rape survivor. Whose flesh was cut open to accommodate. Enormity of steamships driven through. Still reeling, unable to feel pain. (Children, blacks and nonhumans were thought not to.) Size of earnings is still a measure of adulthood. So the infantilised "poor".

a Scold's bridle. Now removed. Though the tongue lacerated and numb. The spirit wandering, homeless, evicted. (The resulting malaise once thought of as an addiction.) Though we were hunted down, our records dispersed, our names forgotten. We know.

an artificial respirator. It gives no thought to the future. It is only here for this breath. Now this one. And now this one. In a sterilized environment. Rendered sterile: unable to reproduce or create life. Kept alive by external forces. That is, by us. This we know well.

bodies deemed disposable. Fed to the apparatus of war. A harvesting site for cannon fodder. Highly skilled in the arts that only love can be competent at. Work which can never be fully repaid with money. Half-heartedly re-branded as "essential." Clap clap clap clap.

ordinary people. Left to our own devices. Mutual aid as the only path to survival. By which I mean tending to those closest to us, as Arvo Pärt said in an interview not reported by the British press. For ages we had forgotten: the point was to care for each other.

a candle. Humbly lit at night. A companion in solitary as we switch off the lights of propaganda. Becoming rich in time for thought, pleasure and conversation. The flame, in its irregularity, grows dim and cool at times, then warms bright again. Just a tempo.

a city. No longer held back. No longer "kept under by the shallowness of her river." No longer drowned by the disquieting depths of prosperity. So-called.

III

The river walks...

Not how we interpret.
       Not when we interrupt.
Not through which simile we
assimilate
  the likeness— takes the figure
of a traffic cone
Its' propellers are esteem
 powered monoliths dredging an absentee sky.

Walk— with a body that does not get swept into many worlds
       does find home, picking dead flowers wherever
it can
       bend its chorus
  —it helps. The softness of the soil and how often the
rain
chooses to reconvene. Razed. Erased. Raised
 both in skin and wound
Skinned and wounded rabid gashing symphony
coalesced on chalked
erasured streets, history unscaffolding the river
side. It is sung —
convert hymns to hums, inhabit dreary dead habits of
streamlike posture when walking this route I was told.

Look towards the walls. The murals I imagined
on Brown street are not there. There is a sieve left on
its embankment. Am I
to be
its refrain?

Agata Maslowska
Sam Healy

You reply to my failed articulations
of home. Your fingers tap on the steering wheel

as if you had no idea what it means
to cross borders.

The horizon sways under the Supermoon,
a man watches it emptying the bins.
I watch it too – its face flowers ice.

My hands are stiff with cold,
I keep looking away in silence,

The distance between you and me
is greater.

> The familiarest stranger. The obscurest brother.
> Out of earshot, who knows. Best not to dwell.

> Best not to tell. Truth weighs a fucking tonne.
> A dozing juggernaut killed six because
> we huddle, or think we want to.

> If wishes were glycoprotein we'd be less inclined
> to beat the system with an "I wish for unlimited wishes".

> Because where's the fun in that?
> No wonder God is depressed.

The anthropomorphized dream of gods
and celestial bodies
brings a sudden but short-lasting relief.

The truth might lie between the constant
searching and getting lost, the way

I do each time I visit
Glasgow, thank god for google maps.

The satellite signal helps me see
what is in front of me as if
my eyes were not enough.

The restless search for home
and by home I mean the fleeting
moment of feeling like myself, the way

I do each time I visit
Glasgow. I don't know why.

By that I mean I do know why
but hard to pin it down,
that feeling, I want to keep it
to myself for now. I hope
you understand.

Keep driving on the left-hand side
avoiding heavy traffic.

We are still in Europe,
even though it feels like
we left it a long time ago.

Ashamed I use you only as a cog, a hub, a switch.
An axle with shabby spokes but
at their tips thicket-greened redbrick hulls, pumping out loss
and longing for a past brutish but more real,
give you a heft your eastern rival cannot match.

Judged on copyright devices, shapes and glowing type,
longstanding viruses of monotony,
yes you wheezing beasts are all the same.
But there's more to you than what's been done
to the sons and daughters of your toiling children.

More to you than prismatic slick oan the watter,
armoured shops, hypodermic quills
with which are scrawled such epistles as
"this place has changed" and
something unintelligible even to pals.

And your yards, silenced families ago?
They'd be silent now anyway.

I'm having text with you
and my life-form changes.
Have I become the city? I feel
larger than life. The city lets the self
come out to itself. The multiple
selves sing the polyphony of Glasgow.

It is not the silence you hear.

In the end no voice remains
suppressed.

The generational trauma echoes
the trauma echoes
through the tissue
of street lights, pavements,
stones and bricks,
and more.

It's through those echoes
that I that we
accept the new, we
accept you
thought you couldn't
hear it.

We are not the sound of
death. On the contrary,
we are not the sound.

And perhaps the emotion
I stir up in you
is also mine.

The boundaries between us
a blur.

Blurs in sound are reverberations.
Like echoes but dirtier,
the signal disintegrating languidly
in transit, losing interest in itself.

We think ourselves – no, I think myself –
principled, constant, built of durable stuff.
The truth is more like unbranded tech bought on the cheap.
When we are – I am – not consciously rehearsing what I
'believe'
I fear I may not know what I believe.
I am a device that works until you need it to.

The replacement bus service,
the all-you-can-eat buffet,
the pound shop bargain.

I pray that's not what I am, when I think of you.
Nor you, Dear Green Place,
when you think of us.
Do you ever think of us
when we traverse you?

Thinking isn't a philosophy of mine,
not in that sense. It's a flow
of light and time I mostly
associate ourselves with.

The movement of our lungs,
asynchronous inhaling and
exhaling woven together
into a city fugue,
an opening out.

We flee each other
through emergency exits
to come together ~
sea waves
sound waves
frothy wondrous
beings.

Some things are constant
like trees growing skyward.

Let me start with our sequence
of notes to illustrate
our meaning.

Keep tapping your rhythm
on our skin – warm asphalt,
tiny gravel, juicy grass,
wet pavement studded with
chewing gum kisses.

Keep melting your words
into ours, away from mono.

What song will you sing to me today?
What language is it in?
No need for a specific answer.
I'm asking out of love.

> But aren't all bets off,
> haven't normal rules ceased to apply?
> This liminal hall we find ourselves in
> (obediently, considerately waiting with
> gargantuan number in hand,
> stuck in a bad dream written by Tim Burton
> and directed by Terry Gilliam,
> while minds without faces decide
> what we are waiting for)
> is a noisy crash of Art Nouveau and synthetic carpet.

You know, the kind that smells of how little
those who made it cared about it. The kind we hate.
Claustrophobic advocacy offices that were once beautiful
banks,
eternal stone shells enclosing disposable yolks.
Emergency exit signs above Rennie Mackintosh doors.
None of it moves me to sing for joy.

A clap, at best.

So easy to miss each other's understanding,
not to universalise nor generalise:
whether a joyful song or disillusioned clapping,
our experiences fall between
dystopia and utopia.

We can't be present at all times
though still alive, hoping
to still be breathing
the day after next,
dreaming a dream
that might belong to fools,
or not.

In cities our perspective
is mostly framed by
tenement windows.
We rarely see

the flat horizon.

Don't forget myopia, that suffix's unholy spirit,
the face that sank a thousand ships.
Helen of Queen Street to Helensburgh.
Nothing weighs her down quite like
being told to buoy up.

But she's fine, you're fine, I'm fine!
We're told by toads to toe the line.
A splintered empire's final straw,
a chalk-scrawled limit: this far, no more.
If we get out alive, we'll thrive.

Is that the vinceremos you're after?
The light looks green, by verdure or disease:
choose the one you please.
No, no! The one that pleases you.
Why does English have such damn trouble
with subject and object?

That's why I'm reading about having no head.
That's why the Anglophone world is half-dead.
I used to love it, but now I'm ashamed
to speak the oppressor's tongue.
I welcome your strange vowels and emphases.
Choose the one you please.

That's the secret, buried in plain sight,
The one I can't make you see:
Self-regulation is not a bad word.
Take what you want, and leave the rest.
Put that self-love to the test.

Hoarders look up from
their hoarding, amen!
It's always now.
It's never then.

In the city of the multiple,
we lose our heads in vowels
which (un)mistakably reveal
our origin, if it matters at all.

The genius loci is a clash of vowels
that shapes our tongues
into soft weapons of rebellion.

English has never been
our mother tongue.
We try to break
the violence inherited
by language.

Let's trip unsettling rhymes.
Let's fight the diphthongs

by getting straight or strate
to the point. Are we
too in-yer-face?

We are now waking up
to once peripheral truth
that our foundations
grow deep roots
in subjugation, in throbbing
pain that flows through
the city's crowded veins.

It's a gyre and we're spinning,
whipped into shape, into smooth dough,
that's how ingredients become cake.
That's how the metropolis spreads for spread's sake.

Payloads good, like music sprouting antlers,
like films in a forest,
getting drunk on the fact that laughs are
unique as fingerprints and have
nothing to do with language.

Or bad, like the religion of ownership:
failing to beat, then joining, Nature's
sublime indifference:
not a good look on Her own disposable pieces.

Our origin (singular) I look at like this:
we – the big We, the whole stinking bunch of us – share a
provenance of improbabilities,
weirdnesses, luck, chance and charm
so unseeably tall
that how we differ
cannot matter at all.

These are imaginings, words forming
surrealities of cities within cities
both true and untrue at once.

Citizens are drilled
to sleepwalk nine
to five, to click or swipe
for pleasure and reward
for their unquestioning
obedience.

I see it as a layer
a mirror to the raw rim
of blinding systems cutting
deep unless we play
their urban tune.

Beneath it all a web
of thoughts and feelings
impossible to catch

in data cookies.
Who is to know and understand
their wealth and meaning?

The city is beneath
the city.

Just for a minute, watch
people walking down
Buchanan Street,
their bodies curious
to explore their greed
for life.
Listen. It's not
all shallow breathing.

Things that are rich:
cakes, people, fuel, voices, lives, histories,
suburbs, colours, odours, soil, cities' cultural heritages.
They can also, of course,
be poor.

A metaphor, never meant literally,
is whispered furtively by each child to the next,
twisted a bit in the telling.
By the time the children are grown
they hold this garbled, breathy myth as gospel.

That's money and god.
That's birthers and truthers,
flat-earthers and breatharians.
That's a homeopathist dying of an underdose,
protesters burning the 5G mast that just
played them cats and sold them hats
and foolishly told them
exactly where it was.

There will soon come a time
when their words will be tested
for antibodies, for viral load,
for follow-through, for truth.

And cities, be their heritage ever so rich,
could end up recast as clots, as egg sacs.
Malignant growths on the planet's pelt.
To be irradiated into harmlessness.

The scars that remain will be objects of
wistful fascination
for the ghosts of our children.

We have been driving for some time now.
The moon gets closer.

The city grows quieter
behind us.

Jim Colquhoun
Jamie McNeill

OF THIRLAGE AND SUCKENERS

1. The pit in which the milk was milked

the octagonal tower/radio shack/omphalos on Brimmer/Browns-muir Hill, being an exact replica of that on Kenmuir Hill to the north, is dedicated to an unnamed local deity (in all likelihood some debased variation of old cernunnos as per) and generations of the Beith & District Young Farmers Association have plighted their troth, given forth their maidenheads and generally cavorted at the bidding of dark forces amidst its roofless gothic splendour

      Oh sunhat pride
Honorific rind breeze
My jellied reliquary out for a run
Woodwind sunbather my skirmish cenotaphs
Bogged vision of the hinterlands
Libationed   yellow-brined floor

Pedigree accredited milk recorded
Hill initiated lost seedsmen
      Sacrificial stairs of the graces
Muscoid inmeats   swarming regularly
Pining agrarian rubbish get amulet
      And lands imminence

Hex bard given the earned gralloch
Coveted their flexor'd radiation
Implies mystagogue revealer of mysteries
Risk marsh wrought canals the mystery solvents
Wander on brae-top   present seed clothing

Rifleman breakwater tone industrial
Way open facility
Hence text   iron-time and moon

The unfathomable dimension
The unexplained mucilage
Brimming mendicants script
Found in the fishing weir
Agree with us   our breeding's been sound

2. A cure for poisoned weapons

Swift sailing   drill cuttings of birds
          Strobes on the open page
Identity of the vessel seems complete
Smother defined ungulate immemorialised
Shivering unit in the aggregate
          Confines gaining something
Exhibiting a volcano-type dependence

          Temperate shrub heathland
Moss hill depicted the serpentry
Hence officiated all masonries hand was a tract
The hushed sheep and all the day's cauldron

Have the given states and eyebrights
Facts are chiels that winna ding
          The sudden lurch
Perfect hint-sense slump forced unwitted
Dark hierophant moon and blellum-talk cavorted
          Revels dread hours

       Special proofreader
The policies break the whilst land
Saucelike catholic breastplate
Pilot hovel access   authorised iron
Await final permission and hushed said
Walkout stickers fencing stagecoach patches

3. Boiled ornament

In the springtime such supplicants shall make their way along the old rakerfield road to the summit of said soggy imminence, and there amidst the sphagnum and the scots pines they choose a mill-bitch to break the quern stone and a dancing circle of thirls and suckeners pass the broken stone through the jug hatch to be hurled into the outsucken* since time immemorial

Bog-moss of unholy williams
Quarter these ecclesiastic lichens
Foaming and cloud road and angulous ditch
Place hunt discharge   excavator lives
Unnamed thoroughfare loudmouth fascias

Vomit still   fell stone excavator
Into that still trough the ruthless ploughshare
In olympian and other mounted incident
Cavorted blood truth set with his set of spoons
Forces scything stone and sacred moon

Milk tones immeasurable embalmed fluorescence
Final milk out a of trader vacuum
Milk sent thereabouts
Seen as individual buyers and customers
The sagas including the end of the britons
The species of autographed pictures

Seen with sodden sickly fauns
Hill waterlilies horsetails cinemax
          Dominated by situation
Here a dog or cowardice
Arrisways   or rainfall in excess of design
Cattle   picturesque scenery   and sauna fun

4. Hosts wandering about stumbling

The burghers smother and destitutes throuther
Broken stone is still spoken is still
Initiate enter this gloomy region
A generation of my seed the presence of dogs
Badly preserved porous remnants

      Red lightful they were driven
Upon this arguing to the end of them
I roll wormcast to have rendered at the proud broods
Radial lines   the gift of quiet rain

Marauding sequence exalting of sneezes and portents
      Animates to keep which magical prevailing
Behalf-moons and berated to examinence
Distribution animal motifs
A Bosch in the moss a Miele in the cairn
     The odour tied in persecutions

Initiated certain phantoms in the figures
Bribed song propitiated with magic
Honey and trefoil and horns flowing with mead

5. Sorrowhawk foam of a purifying circle

I have crawled and embarked
      On an atmospheric environment
A Samsung in the peat a Zanussi in the loch
Deposits of metal castle wall clean your video castles
live and moving brown crab in a blue poly bag

Text the lands of that exorcised variant
Described in stone this was milks recital
Arcane brokered mind the suavity of the last display
Allude the ruddy gem and sprinkling herbs
Reading the markings we must now of the parasite
Defensive future seen form of animals cooled

Sprinkled souls that were making their way
And property policy boards
And weirs in surface waters
      Goals spawning gods fruits spawning
Any arounding this body clothers to the portent
      I stopped at an draughty theocracy

B roads local streets and minor roads
Dominated by forbs of impounding works
My catastrophe architecture awaits diocese

Ferreting hill bidding enclosure
Quarrying blellum-talk in every twain
Pierced door of a closed room
Village had slain their city appeared
The shape of a high-crested hen
Day-dream sweet to that gleaning fair enough

Voice trembling the floodplain stairs
Time-reckoning cycles   narrow the raging water

6. Malevolent serpent week

One particular incident, taking place in may of 1929 in the environs of Threepwood and Brimmer hill is still spoken of in hushed tones amongst those in the know/on the square. Two young men were discovered wandering abroad seemingly melded together by some unholy radiation or other and there was talk of parties of young girls of noble blood abroad on the hill brandishing knives and harrying the sheep whilst divested of their clothing. These and other fell tidings have rendered the Threepwood lands a lost and lonely part of the country, little visited and to this day unexplained lights are regularly seen on the hill and no farmer will quarter his sheep thereabouts.

Aghast in as begot   chalcosite provost
Dug up with the left hand
Overlooked by the vulgar herd
You there special prophet
          Kittled heath-stane
Characteristics of loyalist mildewed glimmer situation

Water stealing radiated site
Increase vehicular movements
Scarify through quartz tone activity
Select franchise hae heavy know
        His welly authorisation
The ghostly ring of picks and shovels
Reverberating and coming apart to bells
A torch lit proper bastard

Their encomium attracts me not when moving
In ghost-like equipoise   of inland safety weaklings
Becoming playback's conspiracy perfectionist
The great nae liberality shingle armistice sculpture
How lingered secrets and itself however others din
Blue polythene crinkling in the quiet
The yonder general future blessings
Of putrid water rising every hour

Subaltern o'clock spelt smother subaltern
Other sucklers will terrorise the grammarian
Special promotion podzol category first breakfast
In ruins and half tumbling with halting step
The gloaming nature's period tell't
Keep sniffing   fox wants some questions
Playback's consequence   rider breakdown

7. Deposition of magic metals

Deciduous and coniferous woodland
      Seaward sexual nectarine
Oh sundry prick sundry my skull centenarians
Wrought moments storeys of mysterious dark day
(How people appear in a mirror
      When passing in front of it)

Goals spawning gobblers front-runners spawning
And green oil boom and without means of birds
She keeps fingerprint   fluffs their purchases
Scripts of certainty and this celtic tribe
And am here pitiably close to their lives
Dormant buds, epicormic shoots and sacrificial growth

The sleep movement in date soil prose
Cut a hole in broad day lighted eyes
Sessile deepening police
As midnight's orange structure puddings
Shrubbery grub ratepayer
      As trowel proximity competitor
Groundwater penance grasslands and lands
Dominated by forbs, mosses or lichens

Eyton dux south the sheep riviera of upricht
Of its diocese and it wasn't a drone
Hush that generosity is potential   their very mist
Pals outside man's angry gateway
Sufferers suckers play footballer hunt of the treetop
Cut down the defensive future seen from animals

8. Ignoble boast

Sredhs and their trampling   drill cuttings of scone
      Shuddering place siccing still
The fodderer established whole house is surrounded
Face explained glowering through cross
With a circle to well manned by thence
      The lime-washed colliers' house

Obscurity and the flux between the earth
Temple tacticians within this lure
Viperous highland   isle agony hillfort
Show ventriloquist chaplaincy
Accord the largest financial foul-up
Make out the the notable oblatary pavement

      Tradesman and the sidetrack walnuts
Islander agnostic hint foul the rug
      The largest milkman cyphers the speedometer
Conversant with the country traversed
Became a greyhound secluded from the moon
      With maceration and sprinkling
And the portion after the sprinkling
Fructifying quality cheerful precious silver

*an immeasurable void, a sump or a drainage ditch.

T. Person
Loll Jung

or I was love, banner up & be lost

I like a city that still
sleeps; a tired city is a low blow.

Aloysius' closed a gap of silence
to pique aural tenders

sometimes I remember
Jana Sterbak who bound

leather carry straps to
a large stone
so you could carry it

here why
now why

I like my city burdened with the weight of books:
literarily holding it down, books stop a city
floating away, or getting too big for its boots. I like a city that
is heavy with all the stories left to tell, that talks
in the dark before bed, a soft murmur *i love you*;

aspiration, it just can't be helped
sucked from stone. The *Co-op*

is hubby material & the column count
high what's it called to be lost in *Cosmopol*

columns or lost in the *Co-op*
for that matter to be lost
between two theatres

> I like a city that is still just a place—not also an idea—
> that has *could-bes* and *maybes*;
> that doesn't talk louder than all its oscillating bits;
> that knows words other cities that exist don't;

that doesn't break
membranes. Give & return

to the centre: column count
increases, cigarette smoke a

gateway that proves travel
Was that a bank?

A theatre?
A warehouse? *The Unit*?
Do I hear talk of an afters?

       I need a city that knows its bounds, remembers what came
              before—the kirk with its hidden hymns, the hillock
                     that harbours words of dead worship—
                          that nods to that-which-is-not-it
                   in amiable acceptance of its not-itness;

torrential sun hits
opaque organelles;
roam the atmosphere, *The Brazen Head*
damnation was it or coronation liberation was it?
Arches tracing skimmed stones, fenced off to
keep their pallor pert. The fizz-eek of green in
Mono

old time, rag time outside the
old metropole was *Scotia*
demolished

a snack while looking
at buildings

I like a city that plays tricks in the light, irises
stuffed with oranges; a city served hot
with the fruits of my labour and the best
memories melting on top. Or a fruit bowl
in Flemish oils, all ochre and rich dusted blues; I—

ironworks tire. *Stereo*
fingers,
samaritans' plaques

like walking
over a hunched back but

thinking of the belly
underneath

like a city that goes well in the night—
sings songs, knows it might be a poem—
if a poem is a city, then this city is whole stanzas
of staccato-beat streets

slowed;
the bus-schedule routine of city's chaos has
seeped
then tricked
its last

best street. Protoplasms
over billboard branches

finger their way through windows
of an old savings bank. Floral *Laurieston*

nest of snakes, fausto. Natural stones,
arranged in a specific order,   for now, if not a poem,
become buildings,   perhaps a map with lines like faults
                                that fold into & across & over
                                appointments like aphorisms; or

the M8 marks the end of decoration
Blue stripes of M8's belly
sorry sparrow, I haven't seen your friend—

                    a chest waiting to be opened with whatever key
                        is at hand, or simply a fresh breath that tracks
                            clouds' routes across scudded skies;

In the *Star Bar*
isn't this the *room de luxe*?
Overlooking shopping corners

at Victoria Cross cogent
as seams;

I like my city locked & loaded, ready to be
opened, undressed, explored; close-read lines
that seem to be run-of-the-mill like the stones used
to grind flours by the river, a scientist
who runs through the green;

The Printing Works [Ref. 5273, HS 33529]
patch of grass is meadow is field is forest

the plannedscape hosts public, picnic, palace
to lie down under the love banner of

Amoeba & Amoeba Ltd. future brand of
love sold by *Ah-me-Bah* to *Ah-You-Bah*

I said, I like a city that moves
at its own pace, an unbidden breeze
through unwittingly open windows;
the pros and cons of living like this;

This Hackintosh life: turn your
flowers to iron and hang them from
your window and let
them rust

sudden dermis presences causes
scaffolding on Egyptian Halls to

collapse and in a
ray of light show

                    The news said it never happened,
                              and then

I made the news into
                    flowers because I was sick of it
sick of the news of flowers, I
                    made that I was into it
I made the news because
                    I was sick and
            into flowers
the news made me into
                    flowers and it
                    was sick
                    flowers made the news, and
                    I was sick of me
the news is sick; instead,
                    simply this:
                    flowers.

Georgi Gill
Gillian Shirreffs

Georgi Gill and Gillian Shirreffs are both from Glasgow where they met. Gillian is completing a DFA at the University of Glasgow, exploring fiction, objects and multiple sclerosis. Georgi is undertaking a PhD at the University of Edinburgh about poetry and multiple sclerosis. In late March 2020, during a highly caffeinated Zoom chat they decided to start two shared writing projects in response to lockdown. 'singular together' is comprised of excerpts from one of these projects in which they take turns to write in a shared document that has become part-journal, part-stream of consciousness, part-pen pal dialogue.

27/3/20

My dreams too have been quarantined; brief
domestic scenes that shudder and fret:

last night, I fished a glass out
of the sink but, soapy, it tumbled

from my fingers to empty space
and slowly, slowly, fell, decelerating

as it slid through heavy air then paused,
suspended in an incessant present,

one inch above the floor. Dream-paralysed,
I watched it, waiting for the crash until

I woke, still helpless, still waiting for the glass to smash.

28/3/20

I'm worried about the postman.
        I'd only just got him to smile at me. It
came from his eyes. Stretched his face wide. Up
until then, in my head, he'd been the grumpy
postman.
                We have dogs, so I understand.
                It was my sign that did it.

Hi!

Could you please leave it at the doorstep?

I have an underlying health condition, so we're trying to be careful about physical contact.

Many thanks!

I knocked on the window. His jaw was in its usual set. He looked wary as he turned his head. As he began to read.

It was early on; before any official lockdown.

Then he smiled the lovely smile I didn't know he had and he set the package down. I mouthed thank you and waved at him.

It's been the other postman for days now. The one I think of as the relief postie: for holidays and busy periods. His face is normally pretty inscrutable. But today he looked worried. And that worry seeped through the glass, through my skin and into my gut.

29/3/20

My wellbeing is increasingly dependent on Daniel Dale's dog

Daily videos and photos of Breezy beam from @ddale8
in Washington, DC, straight into my home. A golden puff
of long-haired chihuahua. An 80s soft-rock wig of a dog.
I'm a cat person but Breezy!!!
#fluffmonster #FurBaby

Stretched on a blanket, belly up, we're all a little Breezy
now, hunkered down, living from food to nap to food
to couch.
#LivingMyBestLife #QuarantinePets

Breezy doesn't know about empty supermarket shelves!
Breezy dances on her hindlegs for treats! Danders back
and forth, jaws snapping for a beefy niblet. Such immediate gratification!
#Oblivious #WhatPanicBuying

Breezy curls up on @DDale8's lap, looks at the camera,
eyes wide and black as a Victorian TB patient on
Belladonna. Petted, adored, adoring. I tell myself I am
not alone in pretending that Breezy adores me too.
#LoveSponge

Tonight Breezy went for a walk! Sniffing the dusty concrete,
the weeds on the sidewalk. Breezy, you are reluctant to walk,
but you stretch, stretch, and breathe the midnight DC air in a
perfect downward facing dog.
#YogaDogs #ShortWalksFeelLongForLittleLegs
Breezy has taken to sitting in a bag and swinging from @ddale8's
hip. Are you depressed, Breezy? Do you feel this imprisonment

deep down inside, beneath your armour of fur? Is this
self-imposed canine lockdown? Breezy, are you OK?
#Worried

3/4/20

The days have been flying in, which makes no sense.
     I keep finding myself noticing it's bedtime. Despite having been unaware of the preceding segments of the day: mornings hurtle; afternoons zip and evenings seem to snap at the heels of both.
     Bedtime stands resolute; stares me in the face.
     I don't love bedtime.
     When I was twelve, or so, I became anxious about it.
     Sleep, to be more precise. The concept of sleep: what it involved; how to initiate it; the other worlds into which I would fall having been subsumed by it.
     I'd had two bad experiences of anaesthesia by this point and I think they joined together to conceive this sleep-worm that burrowed deep.

I would therefore like the days that will fill the gap between now and the world raising its shutters, to be much more morning, or even afternoon.

7/4/20

I've been wondering if, after all this – assuming we can dare to assume there'll be such a thing as an after – I'll go back to washing my hands the old way: a splash of lukewarm or cold water; a scoosh of some lightly fragranced liquid soap; a quick rinse under the still running tap; a hasty pat on a towel that likely needs to be washed more frequently.

I'm worried I won't be able to do it. That I'll always imagine a virus trying its darndest to adhere to the skin of my fingers, thumbs, palms, backs of hands; swarming: a division of tiny invisible ants from the world's tiniest invisible ant tribe.

I do realise there are other more pressing concerns that should probably be occupying the ever-growing worry section of my brain.

8/4/20

In the small, dark, solipsistic hours, worry takes hold while I lose my grip. I freak the fuck out. I freak out about whether I'm getting fat, whether it's a bad idea to monitor my weight and weigh out my calories, whether rekindling old obsessions is a very bad idea or a comforting coping mechanism, whether poetry has lost all meaning, whether I can ever write again, whether the fact I tore a nail is a sign that I'm lacking calcium, whether listening to so much Radiohead is adding to the darkness, whether listening to old school hip-hop is adding to the darkness, whether Glen Campbell's recording of 'Wichita Lineman' is too darn trite or a loneliness classic that is perfect for these times, whether I lack compassion, whether I'm too needy a friend, whether that back upper left molar is twinging, whether I'm too short-tempered these days, whether I dislike some of my friends, whether I dislike a lot of poets, whether they're more or less annoying than other writers, whether I really shouldn't work in poetry, whether I adapted too easily to lockdown, whether I can justifiably pull out of a conference that has been rescheduled online because online conferences are even more excruciating than real world conferences and everything I was going to talk about is now a meaningless waste of time, whether I need to see a dentist, whether I care, whether I am expending an unhealthy quantity of energy thinking about 'Wichita Lineman', whether everybody wakes in the night with the sensation of a rope pulling taut around their necks, whether it's just me.

9/4/20

I'm concerned I might be about to break an unspoken, unwritten rule (and I am such a rule-follower; I fucking love rules, me; I don't, however, love my love of rule-following).

Another thing I love (that in its very declaration is the potentially rule-breaking thing), is this collaborative writing thing we've got going, right here on this here google doc.

It's fucking marvellous.

In a time of worry, it's a fan-fucking-tastic salve.
And the whole having a place to swear thing, that's not just into the dead air of my kitchen, is FUCKING fabulous.

I love the humour; the quirkiness; the mortuary vans that aren't mortuary vans; the poetry; the references to poetry; the statements of the mundane; the lists; the whole fucking shooting match (and the swearing).

And I love having something new to read every day and something new to write. What genius thought this up? Or geniuses? Genii? Who the fuck knows what the plural of genius is, but I now have somewhere to wonder about it. Marvellous.

So, thank you, writing partner; partner in crime; collaborator; co-conspirator; pen pal; epistoler; fellow lover of words.

13/4/20

Typing the date, I realise that it's been a month: a month since I closed my door on the real world.

My last day out was Friday the 13th (of March).

It was the last time I saw my Aunt Rena.

I said goodbye, knowing that it would be.

She died on Saint Patrick's Day.

20/4/20

Today I am fatigued, by which I mean clinically fatigued as opposed to pretentious and tired, although I am that too, always. Today almost every word has to be retyped or corrected as my fingers stumble over keys which oddly won't sit still in their usual configuration. I am the Typo Queen and I wear a crown of wiggly red lines with scrunched up paper jewels glued in place with Tippex.

And I am tired. I am an old T-shirt-turned-floor-cloth that has been wrung out and abandoned to slip down the back of a radiator. I imagine you don't have any floor cloths like that but, take it from me, they are knackered and of limited use to anyone, crusty and unappealing.

I am fatigued and tired by MS but also by the existence of Covid-19 in the world, if not, fortunately, in my bloodstream.

Aren't we all?

I would like to take a day off from it.

Wouldn't we all?

I would be very well behaved on my pandemic holiday. I solemnly promise that I wouldn't go within ten feet of the neighbours; I wouldn't lick door handles; I wouldn't loot the one local pub, which hasn't boarded up its windows, in a desperate attempt to procure tawny port.

No, I'd stay in. I'd wash my hands repeatedly. I'd live a quiet life. To the untrained observer, it would look like I was living a regular lockdown life, but look closely. I would be living a regular fatigue life – a life where I lay on the couch because I physically couldn't do much more, not because the state won't permit me to do more. The knowledge of the deaths, the ventilators, the risks, the protests - all of it would recede for the day. My jaw would soften perceptibly. You'd see the difference if you knew what to look for.

My pandemic holiday would be the chance to be a coward, to roll over and go to sleep in the face of it all.

What would you do if you could take a pandemic holiday? Would you take one?

And yes, the F-G household are regular and enthusiastic cooks and consumers of curry.

Joining the S-D household at a point in the yadda yadda future would be most agreeable!

21/4/20

I prefer your today to mine because your today (which, I do realise would be more properly described as yesterday) was 20/4/20, which would only have been bettered by 20/4/02, which was a lot of yesterdays ago but a beautifully palindromic today, so I'm wistful for it.

I suppose I'll just need to hold out for (hold on until) 22/4/22. Won't that be a marvellous today, although not as brilliant a one as 22/2/22. Now, that will be a today to write home about.

Having said all of that. Your today sounds like it was shite and I'm sorry and I'm sorry I didn't lead with that.

I hope your 21/4/20 is better (despite not being such a good number); less fatigue of the clinical kind whilst having as much as you want of the pretentious lying about on a comfortable and stylish couch kind – which is the only sort of couch on which I imagine you lounging.

I love the plans you have for your pandemic holiday. And I would also take one.

Thank you for the kind offer.

I'd walk each of my three dogs, one at a time, minus the overly tight motorbike helmet I've been using on our current once-a-day-just-before-sunset walks. I'd go on our favourite walk (it carves through the quietest of our neighbouring streets and snakes around the Kelvin). I'd let them each sniff to their heart's content and I'd enjoy the feeling of the warm wind on my face (there will be a warm wind on my pandemic holiday).

Hopeful for better days for all (especially those who have been steeped in the horrors that I only read and worry about) and warm winds and the best sort of lounging on stylish couches. And tawny port.

27/4/20

BEETROOT?

You eat, and enjoy, that blackish-purple bruise of spherically compacted dirt?

I may need to look for a new pen pal. One who doesn't, in addition to loving words, love consuming the Devil's root vegetable, laced with dill (the Devil's herb).

Or, I could just purge the image of you eating it from my mind.

Folding the image in on itself.
Slotting it into a tiny box.
Sealing the tiny box.
Storing the tiny box in the (badly overcrowded) tiny-box-vault in my mind.

Ah. Much better.

30/4/20

In which Georgi once again shows herself to be reclusive and antisocial.

1/5/20

A couple of west coast anomalous Gollums, that's us.
Can we be singular together?
I applaud all the work and the learning to preserve that which must be preserved.
Bravo.
And the prerequisite knowledge of self: of boundaries and sensibilities.
I know myself better now than I did. But it took a while.
My earlier life plays out like a film: laughing, chatting, drinking, dancing.
As do all the attendant nights: waking in

the dark crippled by the memory of laughing and chatting and drinking and dancing.

Wishing I'd been quiet, sober, still.

'singular together' is a fantastic phrase and very probably a better title for this than 'TCTRW'.

Today, I am stalking a delivery driver. Have I told you before about how I stalk delivery drivers? It fits into the category of things I do now that I didn't do in the Before Times.

I ordered my mum a bunch of flowers. They may not be essential but they felt essential. As of this morning, my mother, who lives alone, won't have had a hug for seventy days, not since my brother cuddled her before she went through security at Brisbane Airport on 22 February. I haven't told her I've counted the number of days. She probably knows how long it's been.

My mother is a hugger, so much so that my brother and I joke about her 'Vulcan death grip'. I wish I could give her a hug now, but I can't and so I send a non-essential, completely inadequate bunch of flowers *just to brighten the place up*.

Sending flowers gives me the opportunity to stalk. I follow a tiny green dot on a map of North Yorkshire. The dot symbolises Gary, 'my' delivery driver. (Yodel doesn't tell you the name of your driver, possibly because they are wary of freaks like me, but I've chosen to name him Gary.) I follow Gary in almost real time from the Leeds depot, along the Leeds Road. I wonder if the traffic is heavier today than yesterday; wonder if the sun is bright in North Yorkshire. Gary, do you have to pull down the sun visor? Maybe you're wearing sunglasses? What are you delivering now to Walton Avenue, just off Drury Lane?

Now, you're parked up on Coldbath Road. I can highly recommend the Italian deli. They do lovely fried arancini if you like that sort of thing, although maybe not now. There is a Sainsbury's Local just up the hill and I know from my mum that they're open with painted 2 metre markers on the floor.

I stepped away from the map for a while and now you've moved. Gary, did you drive past Valley Gardens? Is the cherry blossom still out? As you pull a large cardboard box out of your van for drop 27, I imagine cherry blossom petals falling on your hair, a thick head of dark hair, longer than you would like. If you're not a hayfeverish sort, and I don't think that you are, please let a couple of the petals stay in your hair; tiny, faintly fragranced companions as you move from house to house.

12/5/20

Last night, I dreamed I was a shark. Caught and
hoisted onto a ship, belly to tail, I was slit open,
entrails falling onto the deck. This is a variation on a
dream I occasionally have. Dead Shark Georgi does
not feel pain. She does not thrash her tail, desperate
for air. Dead Shark Georgi observes unfolding events
dispassionately. She sees herself as object, pink guts
stinking and glistening on deck. I quite like Dead
Shark Georgi. She has a grip on her own emotions,
although arguably she takes it too far and could be
described as cold, both literally and figuratively.

It's probably Damien Hirst's fault. *The Physical Impossibility of Death in the Mind of Someone Living*,
otherwise known as that Damien Hirst one where
he put a dead shark in a tank. Look at her. Hold your
breath. She's a dead shark and yet she might just snap
her jaws. Flick her tail.

Now that we hear about death every day, I
don't know if *The Physical Impossibility of Death in the
Mind of Someone Living* still holds true. Maybe now
we're at the stage of *The Definite Possibility of Death in
the Mind of Someone Living*?

13/5/20

I had two recurring dreams as a child.

Dream One: Being Buried Alive in Talcum Powder

Talcum powder from a ginormous metal tin.

The tin is orange and is decorated with black botanical wiggles and squiggles.

It's a talc tin from my childhood bathroom (in the house where my parents still live).

In the dream, I can see the orange tin (it can be seen from space, for pity's sake).

In the dream, I can smell the smell of the talc under which Dream Gillian is buried.

I don't like the dank floral smell.

Dream One has taught me three things.

Dream Gillian can be buried alive (might this happen to Awake Gillian?).

Dream Gillian sees colour (orange, at least).

Dream Gillian can smell the dank floral smell of orange-tinned talc whilst asleep.

Orange-tinned talc on a shelf in a room next door.

Dream Two: Being Pursued by a Headless Horde

The creatures that chase me have human bodies.

The creatures that chase me don't have human heads.

In place of a human head is an arrangement of masks.

This is hard for Awake Gillian to explain.

Imagine a rod inserted into each human throat.

Attached to this rod are multiple flat masks that depict different faces.

Each horde member is able to flip through their masks at will.

Dream Two has taught me three things.

Dream Gillian can run.

Like Awake Gillian, Dream Gillian can't run fast enough.

Dream Gillian would very much like the *Realm of Sleep* to be given an upgrade.

In *Realm of Sleep Mark Two* there would be a clearly marked escape hatch.

Nia Benchimol
Rhian Williams

The quality of collaboration may be strained.
Constrained. We've found that when one of you
has been around for less than   six years,
collaboration tends not to   take the
form of a decision. Or a   project. Our
collaborations are not   discrete. Or
discreet. Living   resolves
into collaboration. It's   a bit
ecological. Our setting.   Default.

Like when I am reading Callie Gardner's
Naturally It Is Not. in bed at Mum and
Dad's house and you come and find
me and climb in and start pointing
out all the words you can read and
these operate as an algorithm that
meshes with Callie's and the words
pop and stretch and I can't not see
them and the poem snags and emerges through
and around that net. The anthology I'm working
on keeps feeling like   your list picture of
SCIENCE: SCIENCE:
SCIENE;   SCIENE; SCENE;
SCENEN: SSCENE: ENECS:
eNES: eNECS.   In a good way.

    Do you know   how you get rain?
There's these little people that are little drops, and
   they have a big house and there are lots of stairs

around. They are very long stairs that go round
and round and round, but then they jump off a
diving board, but they have to   wear special
glasses to make raindrops   and then
they go down and down   and down
and that's rain coming   down as
raindrops, with tiny   people with
drops.

It is 1204 steps from our door to the school,
according to my phone. 2069 if we go the river
way. Straight lines or curvy lines. Now
we walk in loops and spirals. A double
helix converged. Always stuck together
(with tape and glue), we never separate,
one walking body, a very long and
provisional strand (pulled forward by the
dogs, dragged backwards by the child)
stretching around the river, never dropping
hands. Have we become a COVID-19 RNA
thing? Provisional, synthesised from something
else, *en route* to degradation and recycling.

Sometimes people walk around in circles
when they're thinking. It's too deep for me.
I'm never going to throw my key in there. I
just saw a plastic packet of tissues on the floor,
but the people threw it away when they hadn't
even finished it yet. Why does that happen? I just
saw a wee dog on a sign! The Billies are in their

banana boots. I'm not like anyone else in life; I
take thousands of pieces.

That whole book of the writing is a
poem. The people write inside
whole poems and the title is a
poem. *I am the Seed that Grew the
Tree.*

Rrr----iiiii----eye?----iii, ivv,---vvv----eerrrrrr.
River. R*i*ver. Oh. *River.* Yeah, English is
fucking difficult to learn to read. Even the easy
words. 'The hill was   one of the many
drumlins, which   were formed by
ancient   glaciation which
shaped the   landscape in and
around   Glasgow. The
exposed rear of   the house was
protected from   the prevailing westerly
winds by a ring of beech trees.' We don't climb
the hill anymore. Or even see it.

Nigel said that there was a sugar factory down by
the river which   was there when he was
little. He said   that one day it had an
explosion and   all the kids around in
the schools   were asked to come
down and   eat up all the sugar. I
wish I was   there that day. There
isn't   anything about it on the
internet   though.

145

I'm so sorry this is happening to you. I'm so sorry this is happening to me. I am so sad. Is it beautiful? Oh to be in Glasgow, now that April's here. Truer than we ever knew. This river, those buds, this stiff breeze, our green light. Is also everything.

And that's when we get to the bit where Coco is going to open her café that only sells carrots and ginger nut biscuits. And she's going to be so excited when she eats them that trumpets will

come out of her ears and rainbows will be all around her and at the end she will burp out the whole milky way.

Denise Bonetti
Jamie Bolland

Another Zombie Nerfland

Delivered

Today 18:44

The world won't shrink
for dwarves-they have
to build stilts-two
pieces of wood-some
duct tape-and they're
off

Score by Edwin Stevens
Photographs by Alice de Bourg

After an unfortunate typo, I managed to screw things up badly enough that my first large world test had hundreds of artists, split into just three gigantic world-wide societies based on their art form, but I've put some controls on size and made them mix together properly again. It would have been bad to suddenly have two hundred dancers show up at the fort and ask for drinks after a performance you haven't even seen.

A zombie nerf has arrived. [Hello] The animated critters no longer block, dodge, parry, wrestle or sprint, and they do charging attacks whenever possible. Zombies no longer receive positive defence adjustments for body part types, and they don't seek or prevent combat opportunities. Their strength bonus has been reduced. Severing all non-smashed heads on a zombie kills it (smashing heads already worked in previous iterations), and severing or smashing any working grasp on a headless zombie kills it. Zombies can still be reanimated if they have a working grasp, and they still have some undue benefits they share with wild animals (you should be able to strike or stop many unarmed attacks with weapons), but it is much better than it was. I still sometimes get those invincible unsmashable zombie heads. I'll try to figure that out. Let me figure that out.

It wasn't strictly necessary, as usual, but we're adding a few more cover identities to be used by agents sneaking into towns to collect information (they can also use the existing train of artist, scholar and wrestler professions as cover). In order for the agents not to stick out for the player, their cover professions need to be held by real counterparts. So there'll be prophets, pilgrims, monks, peddlers and petty criminals. They won't get many mechanics, but they'll be around. The stuff we do add for them has a secondary purpose to set the stage for the myth release -- the prophecies are stored in a way which aligns with the poetry generator we wrote (though that's not coming in yet), and it also relates to an expanded language framework (that's not coming in yet either). It should be good to toy around with those ideas a bit first before we get to the full implementation.

Fixed crash bug from saving while somebody is falling down a property ladder, made items drop when a ramp is dug out beneath them, stopped dig designations from persisting on caved-in spaces, stopped soldiers from pilfering food from caravans for their cute little backpacks, allowed units that can't find a bed to rest with a wee drink and a snack, added option for dwarfort.exe priority, stopped farms from reset-ting to earlier seasons, handled floor placement for walls constructed below melting liquids

parallel-path: in my dream last night I was a drag queen named miss scampy paella and I did live stand up at the VMAs in a cassandra goth outfit

Removed adamantite skills from startup, removed woodcutting from unit-type determining skills *again*, made farms restrict based on knowledge and seasons, changed counter mesh options to less opaque bougie swatches, offered add in zero-hour option, added demand counter, changed how box permissions work (more lenient), made them care about fabric softness more, made mood dwarves not mood boards, chest checks and other things, added foreign material preferences [although carrara marble forcefully overwritten]

Made [tantrum] happiness thoughts, fixed cage crash bug, improved edges of map (SoundSurveyEnabledTrue), fixed capricious occupancy bug in starting layout, changed evalorder loop order to make things go faster and harder, created a less ideologically-implicated viewscreen system, revamped the status screen to [shiny], made viewbuildings(), improved viewjobs(), did stock pile viewing, handled viewproblem with nemesis containers, made the job kill exception system, gave viewstores() zoom to item zoom to item zoom to item

We're done with the list -- I'm going to have to push off rumour display changes for a bit, since I spent the day I set aside for that chasing crash bugs instead. The crash bugs were squished though, so I'm happy enough with the outcome. We're doing release mode tests now and going through the churn of tweaks that happens before it's ready enough to go. There will still be plenty of issues left for you to enjoy, along with all the new stuff. Never fear the go-live. Fix fix fix, fix fix fix. Fix.

Fixed a bug with haunting, added support for material and item+mat piles, fixed cursed aura on particularly sticky bug, lack of aura on another, did startup dwarfgen screen, changed map scrolling, fixed crash bug with charred sheets, more specific barrels, tantrums etc
Sped up pile code, fixed water bugs, changed how accounts obscure values if no nobles are within a [100unit] radius, no potash/coal bar buildings at work, changed how bin permissions work,
safecage_vermin was doing cages and channels, fixed seed bug, fixed issues with item ownership and pickup chest items, fixed straps on fluffy backpacks, found bugs inside, emoji crestfallen sites
Bag support for seeds, leaves, want bins, bronies logjam fix, care for animals, other bug fixes, care for squat release
More bugs, implemented lots of tweak features
More bugs and other tweaks
More bugs, and other freaks
More bugs, dm, more bugs
More bugs
More bugs

Major bug fixes:
Stopped certain situations where you could be
stuck in the air above certain tiles thinking about
cute and fluffy puppies
Fixed a few problems with necromancers
attacking (and generally being killed by) their
zombies
Fixed crash involving squads and minimap
Stopped dwarf from stressing out over the same
wound forever
Stopped certain inaccessible jobs from blocking
lower priority ones
I have never played cricket and I fucking hate lemons

Fixed farming and web collection bugs,
other bugs - I truly believe in bugs() cretinous bugs,
geology bugs, changed bridges, changed ways
Worked on diplomacy bugs, did plot arcs, call
back option from sad dwarf in the corner
Worked on diplomacy bugs, more plot arcs.
Finished trade requests, fixed some ownership
bugs, looking to enhance in times of crisis - if
dollar will allow
privacy laws fixed - how big is your house;)
Worked on trade, worked out diplomacy flow.
Made diplomacy events
Made diplomats into realtors

Restructured diplomacy plan

Added basic histories, added nemeses
Improved magic framework, improved daily feed
of stories, added artefact possession back in,
allowing owners prestige to increase with
conceptual weight of item
improved artefact creation to ensure lowest price
for the rich. Finished unit sales, ponds, king
arrival, adamantite mandates, some endgame
prep. Started unit sales. Barlanark fax alert
soundtrack has been toggled on

Other bug tweaks
Made removal of trees, sickening
Stopped worker peeing next to construction job
Tentatively fixed curtains in the living room
before arrival of auntie
Tentatively fixed broken sound on answering
machine
Fixed that problem with the water thing
Drawn friends disappearing when they cross the
 z=0 boundary

Handled items better, with more care - love even
merchants bring pets for sale
Added better cages, bonus retrieval of small pets,
pet antics, pet coughs - better pet ownership, long
term warranty, insurance etc added. Fixed death,
in the short to long term
lost problems for merchants
Fixed a bunch of merchant dogs, fixed the
wagon-shitting luggage problem
Fixed the military civilian, added activation
squad, made soldiers stop working
Added basic instruments and toys
Finished incarceration
Continued incarceration
Started incarceration
Created sheriff, hamster and fortress dogguard
Finished burial
Started burial
Inputted giant job list
Coalesced noble/spleen manager plans, started
blue screen black
New glass stuff, look command
shuffle

Fixed error with underground poops in small forts not appearing (why)

Stopped moody boys from going outside of burrows

Increased "fighting" skill in the garage

Stopped random creature proboscis from sometimes messing up poison attacks

Made gel faces for pets on animal screen properly

Fixed display problem with agreement conclusion dates

Added error logs for missing materials set to defaults, fixed various scratch cards

Haha

Rosie Roberts
Mark Briggs

DOGSBODY/GREYMATTER

I get out of the car feet first and run to the door

        It's the first day of autumn

run to the grass, relieve myself

        Sorry I had an ice cube in my
  mouth.

a rhythmic city pigeon, we're in

        I'll start again
        It's the first day of autumn

pat my head

        You want to wrap up warm

pat it

        You want to feel the cold air on
  your face

pat my head
pat it

The fresh early autumn air

pat it
pat it
pat it

You want to feel it against your
face

I'm here! Your home! I'm here!

You want to go be outside, to go
for a walk

'fetch'

In the brisk early Autumn air
You have your boots
Your jacket, a hat, some gloves

Ok, I'm going, I've done the work, I'm back!

You are wrapped up warm

reward?

It's a Sunday

I've got a dogsbody and I'm not afraid to use it

                    You want to experience that
              feeling of autumn

In the bath I'm so tiny, shaking, stop moving

                    The feeling of the fresh autumn
          air and being wrapped up warm

Rub my head into carpet, water roaring in my
ears

                    In your jacket, a hat, some gloves

                    There's that early morning mist
          that you seem to only get in
autumn

                    When you take a breath and
          breathe out you can see it
                    You can see your own breath

              Because it's cold

scritch scritch scritch, so loud on the gallery grey
concrete floor, smells toxic, prefer green grass
and forest

we are companions

        And you're in your jacket, a hat,
   and some gloves

we are companions

        And you're all wrapped up warm

we are companions

        And you can see your own breath

we are companions

        It's misty out; that early morning
     mist that you only get in autumn

we look so good together online

dichotomy – I don't want to manipulate you
because I love you / but I want to manipulate
you because I want rewards

explosions in the night
inconsolable I piss on the floor
is it over? is it over?

It's a Sunday you have nothing
else to do

You want to be outside, walking
in the city in that early morning
mist, where you can see your
own breath... all wrapped up
warm... In your jacket, a hat, and
some gloves

You want to drive out of town,
somewhere close by, somewhere
where you can walk in that early
morning mist, where you can see
your own breath...all wrapped up
warm...In your jacket, a hat and
some gloves

A morning stroll

Morning, morning, oh getting on with work, I'll
be warm toes

Morning, morning, help me out, I want to go out,
will you take me out

Morning, morning, there's a letter, you did not get
it, I destroyed it

A Sunday morning stroll, and it's
the first cold snap of
autumn...you want to see your
own breath and be all wrapped
up warm. You want to be outside
walking in that early morning
mist

I want your love

So, you take a drive, get out of
town, somewhere close by, the
sea perhaps?

I want your love

A Sunday morning stroll by the
sea

I want your love

The cold sea air against your
face, the taste of salt on your lips

I want your love

You want to see your own breath
and be all wrapped up warm

I want your love

Walking in that early morning
mist, the autumn mist that comes
in off the sea

your love

A Sunday morning stroll. The
first cold snap of autumn...you
want to see your own breath and
be all wrapped up warm... In
your jacket, a hat, and some
gloves

your love, your love

The cold sea air against your
face, the taste of salt on your lips

I want your love

You want to walk by the wooden
beach huts coloured candyfloss
pinks and sunset reds and rich
navy blues

I want your love

                You want to walk upon the
          reinforced concrete promenade
that meets the sand and shingle
of the beach

your love, your love

                 You want to walk up to where
          the sea meets the sand and
shingle of the beach and feel the
cold sea air against your face, the
taste of salt on your lips

                  The high tide of an early autumn
            Sunday morning, the low riding
waves lapping against the sand
and shingle

Treat me fairly please. I do so much around here
too. I have checked all the corners for enemies
and food. Everybody loves us because we are so
gentle.

                  The first cold snap of autumn,
           you can see your own breath and
are all wrapped up warm in your

jacket, a hat and some gloves.
The cold sea air against your face
the taste of salt on your lips

                      And you're in the car, the sound
              of the sea ahead of you. You can
see your own breath. Your hands
are cold and you put them under
your armpits. You can see your
own breath and the windows mist
up
That woman is looking down on us, she doesn't
like us, because she is afraid of us but we don't
know why, we have never seen her before and she
is scared of us, she doesn't like us because we
don't shit inside, we like to shit outside

                    You want to walk by the wooden
            beach huts coloured candyfloss
pinks, sunset reds and rich navy
blues. You want to walk upon the
reinforced concrete promenade
that meets the sand and shingle
of the beach

everybody hates us because we are scared and
shouting about it shouting shouting shouting,

panic, pause, hide

                        You want to walk up to where
                the sea meets the sand and
shingle and feel the cold sea air
against your face, taste the salt on
your lips

careful you can't trust the door careful because
you cant trust that man careful because I can hear
a noise careful because bright lights don't make
sense careful because there are loud
unexplainable explosions careful because
someone is upstairs shouting at their partner
careful because in this big white space we can't
relax careful because
if you leave me too long, I will destroy all your
things

                        You can see your own breath and
                the windows mist up and with
your finger your write the word
H E L P on the inside of the car
door window

                        Your hands are cold and you put
                them under your armpits

                    You can see your own breath and
            the windows mist up and with
your finger you write the word
H E L P on the inside of the car
door window

                    It's the first cold snap of
            autumn...and you're all wrapped
up warm in your jacket, a hat and
some gloves. You can see your
own breath and the windows
mist up and with your finger your
write the word H E L P on the
inside of the car door window

                    You write the letter H then the
            letter E and as you write the letter
L the driver reaches across you
and pulls open the car door
handle
when we weep, we get into bed and fall asleep,
after we go up and down a mountain and get into
bed and sleep for sixteen hours and get up in the
evening and eat biscuits sitting on the floor

                    It's the first cold snap of
            autumn...and you're all wrapped

up warm in your jacket, a hat and
some gloves and you can see
your own breath and you can feel
the cold sea air against your face
the taste of salt on your lips. You
can hear the sea beyond the
wooden beach huts coloured
candyfloss pinks, sunset reds and
rich navy blues

when we rejoice, we run through the woods
howling, in the summer we swim in salty sea then
paddle back to shore and roll around sandy and
wild

                        You can hear the sea beyond the
                reinforced concrete promenade
that meets the sand and shingle
of the beach, the high tide of this
early autumn Sunday morning,
the low riding waves lapping
against the sand and shingle

In the winter our hair is muddy and our brain is
muddy and we behave badly and people see and
they say NO BAD DOG and, in the spring, we
sniff buttercups and lie in the tenement garden in

the grass or on a rug

always attendant for bin rats

                    You know what

Fuck it

                    On my desk I have a large water
                jug that I drink from... it's a
normal type of jug and I use it as   a
drinking glass and it also makes   a cool
sound when I rub my   finger on
it, but it's like really   large...
It's become this feature   on my
desk, because of its size,
so when my colleagues at work
walk by they can't help but to
comment

"Hey, that's a large water jug"

                    I know its large because it's my
                water jug, sitting on my desk. It
            takes up a lot of space, and they
            say

"Hey, that's a large water jug"

                    And I take a drink from this large
                    water jug, my water jug sat on
          my desk and they say

"Hey that's a large water jug"

                    I'm drinking from this jug with
          two fucking hands and they say

"Hey that's a large water jug"

                    Then I spit on the floor and they
          say

"Hey that's a large water jug".

Jane Goldman

COLLABORATION POEMS

WRITING AND TEXT: A LECTURE

for paddy lyons 25 october 2017

prelude
'his criticism is poetry'
wrote philip hobsbaum
of paddy lyons his lectures

        too say i-i so in sway to the tilt
        and the lilt of lapidary lyons
        falling back like a student
        of saussure on the notes
        (these days it's iphones
        the equally defective tool
        of poor faulty amanuenses)
        i-i swoon to his sashaying wit
        in lecture room café or bar
        here he is in his swan-song
        addressing the matter of text

i. narrative-ideology-text
narrative is the point where
the word *and* changes and becomes
the word *because* narrative pre-
supposes cause and effect (that's
my belief it may not be yours)
whereas ideology is to do

> with assumptions assumptions
> are not the same as beliefs
> we may discover a dog's
> assumptions but not a dog's
> beliefs dogs make assumptions
> about the way the world wags
> ideology asks us to consider
> the kind of assumptions behind
> writing like the shift from rural
> dynastic marriages to urban
> nuclear ones that spurred milton's
> great meditations on marriage
> in paradise lost ideology
> asks us to consider the kind
> of assumptions a text entertained
> or combatted but the word text

shifts attention from what produces
writing to what is in front of us

on page or stage—the product
if you like the methods whereby
the text proceeds its composition
how is the thing composed if
we were to say one word to sum
it all up that word would be *how*
how is it made how does it differ
how does the good soldier work
as a novel does it work in
the same way or a different way
from geek love or in the cage
how does a drama text work
a drama text works on the stage
it doesn't work as a book or
maybe it does as well
a play is made for the stage
not for the book what *is* the book
of a play certainly from the early

> period marlow ben jonson congreve
> books of plays were issued in public
> after the play had a good innings
> on the stage and the play text
> was first issued as a souvenir
> to be bought after the show

ii. education

plays of the sixteenth seventeenth
centuries in other words weren't
put into print to be read by studious
little people looking to get

b grades or c grades they weren't
anything to do with education and grades
education doesn't involve itself in grades
really until after i would say eighteen
hundred it was pass or fail before then
all this fluttering around after grades
that's very much late twentieth twenty-
first century nonsense it has nothing
to do really with the processes
of education the processes
of education are about
learning and expanding whereas
grading is all about solidifying
your grades have nothing to do
with the education you're getting
you'll find in later life when you're
away from here that you will think
about your education and how
you got it what you learn
that's what you'll stay with

iii. shuttle

one move we make is close
reading looking word for word
at the language of a piece
of writing the other thing
we do is we move to big

> theory big speculation large
> cultural questions about writing
> and we try and shuttle between
> on the one hand the close reading
> on the other hand the big
> speculation this is basic
> to what you learn in university

what you learn in any subject
in the university is to
become increasingly supple
increasingly nimble of mind
in that shuttling between
the particular and the general
this is the basis of all
university education
you don't deal only
with the particular
you don't deal only
with the general
the mind has to move

has to be able to move
between one and the other

iv. secondary reading

you ask about so called secondary
reading what is worth your while
is the wilde essay and the brecht
piece—read alain badiou on
the century roger fowler's
dictionary of modern critical
terms catherine belsey's textual
practice erich auerbach's mimesis
a long book you can dip into

i'll tell you what i think can
be a well of poison is project
muse and j-stor i find a lot
of the criticism that people
look up on search engines
on the internet very sad
i find it to do with smallness
of mind i find it only
to do with the specifics
they're really looking for somebody
else to do the reading because
they don't know how to read
is what i think (i can say this

i'm retiring in september)
i think there's a load of shite
going on in english literature
from people who can't read
a book or don't want to read
a book they're only interested
in grades they don't want to read
i wish they'd go and do something
useful like plumbing or electricity
or nuclear physics or brain surgery
so called secondary reading is a set
of traps that get in the way of

> what is often a faltering thing
> independent thinking
> william blake said if the fool
> would persist in his folly he too
> would become wise looking up

j-stor is to do with wanting
an outcome before you've done
the work to get it it's wanting
it in some premature way

> you know what i'd say
> i'd say read books

coda

and i-i say yes let's read books
by all means read them we must
but listen as i-i do with lyons
for where *and* becomes *because*

> listen with lyons he's with woolf
> and more often with barthes
> in knowing the reader to be
> the writer's fellow-worker
> and accomplice he is often
> this reader's fellow-worker
> and accomplice and perhaps
> he is sometimes yours too
> i-i hear the lilt and the tilt
> of lyons in so many books
> coaxing a faltering thing
> into thinking like dancing

listen with lyons he's with gentle
spinoza who took it as axiomatic
that the word 'dog' cannot bark
that to take the word for the thing -
hearing 'dog' bark - is to mangle
an egalitarian liberty of language
a dialogical democracy of desire
there in a poetry of restlessness
of intelligent and vigorous doubt

to take just one nimble example
released out of rochester by
lyons who proffers the reader
a key that unlocks the back door
to duchesses who fuck or are fucked
with porters and car-men—and if

       this is talk too uncouth says he
       citing the great william empson
       to be entertained by 'such as
       a university professor
       or a puritan preacher' and thus
       cannot be accommodated
       within english literature
       a question arises (it is *the*
       crucial big question i-i think
       set by lyons one at any rate
       that has stuck with me):

          how far
are the boundaries of what is
or is not 'literature'
instituted on a class bias
that disallows levelling?

            how far
       are the boundaries of what is
       or is not 'literature'

        instituted on a class bias
        that disallows levelling?

what a beautifully plain cut
big critical question from this
virtuoso poet accomplice
and he has so many more
but this is the one that i-i hear
whenever i-i am reading a book
yes i-i know full well the word
'dog' cannot bark but often
when i-i am reading a book
i-i really do hear lyons roar

SIX FROM THE TWELVE

ONE: Jane Goldman, Tessa Berring, and JL Williams:

Peculiar Fibres Of My Being

What are we looking at?

What are we ever looking at?

Do you want poetry? Or someone alive?

Poppy seeds in the warm loaf

A little drink in the side room

It aches, wait, oh I don't know

Let me stretch (let me love!) to an edge.
                              (**Tessa Berring**)

a little drink in the side room

sex can bring things down to earth

she died there eaten by foxes

said love all possible bodies

there's no savings and no mirror

am just mobilising now we

didn't stay with the exhibition
                    (**Jane Goldman**)

it's only a little ways to the end of the line

when I took out the jacket from last summer it
said, 'the best is yet to come'

I wondered, kissing him, who'd finally taught
him how to kiss

it didn't take long for this moon to delineate

she died there eaten by foxes
many do, it's the done thing now

I lie in bed naked feeling the universe expand
    (**JL Williams**)

What I'm trying to say is I want to wrap you around me

The words for this are different but all over the world the
    action is the same

I lie down on you I fold you over me I fold you over me

Babies, brides, corpses - we all know this feeling

The sun is a kind of torn open burning breast

There I saw your lips opening just like mine

No one coughed no one even said a word
    (**JL Williams**)

there's nothing to say of the photograph now

how quickly a landing page disappears what

is it exactly to openly reference real life people

when the reality of our rage is this grim failure

to expend our labour on its own material as cities

burn world events hang loosely suspended it is

there i-i saw your lips opening just like mine
                    (**Jane Goldman**)

TWO: Lila Matsumoto and Jane Goldman:

Trombone

      Her mother telephoned to say that her
grandmother had made her a blouse
      with snap buttons: two metal discs, one
with a protruding lip and the other
      with a groove, which interlocked to hold
the fabric together. In order to secure
      the snap buttons, her mother said, your
grandmother had to hammer them in.
      What's more, to ensure the buttons were
in place, they had to be hammered
      over a hard surface. So she hammered the
buttons over a cast-iron pot, but
      this made a terrible noise. She worried
about the neighbours. The only thing
      to do, she decided, was to travel to the
countryside where she could hammer
      in peace. She boarded a bus into the city.
She lived in the capital of the country,
      a sprawling megalopolis. Downtown she
changed to a bus heading to the foot
      of a famous mountain and a forest. The
journey took her over two hours. Once
      she disembarked, she realised she was
surrounded by tourists who were eagerly

exploring the forest, the late spring sun
hot on their faces and legs. She had to
walk far away from them, which was
more difficult than she imagined. She would
find an unpeopled place, only to see
someone's head bobbing up the path, or some
children running wild, laughing,
emerging from nowhere. Finally, after an hour,
she found a secluded spot by a river. She
took the blouse out of her bag, and the
hammer, and began to hit the buttons on
top of a large flat rock. Suddenly she was
aware that someone was watching her.
About twenty feet away, she could see a
figure, washing something vigorously in
the river. It was a raccoon, her mother said
on the phone, washing a watch in the
fast-running water.

(Lila Matsumoto)

tromboon

hot on a wild laughing capital
a dog this mad about only a thing
that is not a thing at all but a living
organism as a dog is and this dog
ran off and finally found a spot far
away and this dog took out a bag and in it
was a sprawling gal that's right a sprawl
of a girl you could say and so truly truly
not a thing as difficult tourists would know
but would not want to know but
a not-thing is for a dog to undo
of any last bit of its quiddity
pulling out of this surrounding bag
fabric (no cat) with snap buttons a task about

       as difficult as tourists watching
       a fast-running war taking a bus
       down town for food or a child running down
       a famous mountain not knowing it was
       a famous mountain but just running wild
       laughing down a mountain but can a child
       run down a mountain not knowing anything
       for a dog knows a sprawling gal is not
       a thing but a kind of dog any dog
       is also a bitch (i-i ask you did
       you think of this dog as a bitch?) it is
       so in your world and so in this world too

a bitch too in fabric with snap buttons
(i-i know i-i am i-i for this gal knows i-i)
buttons go snap snap now round this girl
gal who sprawls who barks fuck this
war who sobs who howls watching
difficult tourists war-chasing tourists
who insist on a war but at this cast
iron hour of war insist on boarding
a bus to a city any polity will do
tool for comfort food oblivion of sorts
wanting it now now that war is boring
war is just a boring tour but knowing too
i-i am wanting my comfort food now
this war is just so boring full knowing
just as a raccoon mid-burn full knows
a thing or two is missing from this
vista knows as a fox jumps a lazy
dog a thing of sorts is missing can
still say fuck you and voilà
i-i so just know i-i am in this world
and i-i am washing this (watch)
(**Jane Goldman**)

THREE: Anne Laure Coxam and Jane Goldman:

Survivors

A text "nice to see you over the vegetables!" In my recollection we were, in the supermarket, over all sorts of creams (single, double, fraîche etc.) or maybe over the fish and shells on offer. I always notice the differences between my memories and people's account of circumstances. Is it only me who notices?

I typed "buy octopus Edinburgh" in Google. I have thousands of results including "buy whole octopus on line" and "the 15 best places for octopus in Edinburgh" and "Buy fresh octopus online / locally caught / UK delivery" and (on page 2) "buy now" about an octopus bracelet.

Nicky put on his cream jacket, he's going out with his daughter, he asks me if I want something. Implicitly he asks me if I want something from the outside world.
"Maybe you could go to Eddie's seafood market, see if they have octopus."

I think the text said "nice to see you over the vegetables!" because there were a lot of them in my basket. I remember red peppers and spring onions.

I clicked on Eddie's seafood market website and I
shouted "Nicky! Don't go
to Eddie's seafood market, they are shut until the 17th."

I read a book by a woman who survived the wreck of the
yacht where she was employed. She survived, with one of her
companions, after days in a lifeboat in the Atlantic Ocean and
its long dark nights. They covered themselves with algae to
keep warm, there were small crabs in the algae. She saw sharks
eating the two other members of the crew, she saw the sea red
with their blood.

"How long will you be?"
"I don't know, trying to find octopus."
"I'm waiting for you. For lunch."

In my household, we are under the water even if the roof was
fixed. We are drowning.

In Waitrose, on a poster opposite the till, Moira Howie, Partner & Manager Nutrition & Health, stands next to the yogurts,
smiling, her arms alongside her body. I met a couple called
Howie, they were working in Waitrose too. Does the Howie
family own Waitrose?

Text to Nicky "maybe in a Spanish deli for the octopus (emoji
of an octopus) xxx", Nicky texts back "good idea. xxx"

A couple was walking behind us in the street, very near us, shouting their conversation in our ears. They were very loud, it was painful. When they walked passed us, I asked Nicky "why are these people so loud?"

The butcher was shut today.
Family wedding.

Tesco Magazine
"Llove cake
If the kids have a birthday coming up or Bake off just has you craving cake, try the fun new vanilla sponge **Lucky the Llama Cake**"
I'm reading it out loud to Nicky who says "this makes me wonder if the world is real."

This morning a wasp was in the bedroom, the only alive animal seen in four days apart from the rabbits near the airport and dogs.

This morning I missed a swim with Amanda and Sophie in Portobello because I'm bleeding. But really, I like to swim in rivers.

Seafood, fish and sea always upset me a little. I'm longing for rivers, for the smell of silt, for the emptiness of the shore. But I rarely leave Bruntsfield and I'm bleeding and I'm sobbing and I'm trembling regularly and fiercely like an animal who dreams.

(**Anne Laure Coxam**)

a supermarket in midlothian

 in the moment in the memories tasting dark and
blood frozen
i-i was i-i confess already at an open window
texting myself

musing among the vegetables was that it but
preferring cauliflowers
to men in some aisle of a neon fruit supermarket
where i-i like to

loiter alone and palely shopping yes for peachy
images on the qui vive for poets
and so wanting when i-i saw you silent so
delicately musing over the frozen
 fish to ask you when i-i saw you silent so
delicately musing there and then
anne laure what were you doing down by the
watermelons and with what delicacy

not wishing to make a lonely old grubber of either
of us thinking too of bacon's
vincent on his way to work of all that delicacy
want and market a hungry market

in which the sea corridors (it crabs) and essential
artichokes double in price
i-i was searching in the crème fraîche aisles for a
new queer courage-teacher

your poem has made me think what thoughts
tonight of these our animal days
(there are no other) of the animal that therefore i-i
am and i-i follow

(**Jane Goldman**)

FOUR: Alice Tarbuck and Jane Goldman:

1)
It is the small way you change
on the phone, your voice
a way of holding me
and asking to be held.
We have decided we cannot live without
one another, in the ordinary, life changing way
neither of us have ever decided anything else.

2)
Archways, doorways
those beaded curtains that slither,
I want to walk out, in my dreams
all i do is leave, leave, leave.

3)
Look at the good new things.
Look at the good new, brand new
I never lacked for want before and now
No objects charm me. Take my old
Worn, soft, sweet things.

(**Alice Tarbuck**)

some objects will charm

objects in this moment of
incoming and disappearing
meanings make for us a now
of intelligibility that anchors
our historicity the cat plays

toss and chase
with the cat-nip
laden sky-blue
impossibly feathery toy
mouse skidding the whole length of the hall
becoming an habitual
image suffusing
one possible

future anterior
when we will
have hooked this
tatty eviscerated
chimera out
out from the dusty
underbed
when we will
have said this
this is what she played with
in the time of the covid quarantine

and the lying faces of shameless politicians
nightly pledging their phantom protection
(**Jane Goldman**)

FIVE: Theresa Muñoz and Jane Goldman:

White hallways

I get lost in white hallways, art galleries mostly,
struck by framed bodies unfolding
when flashback is a breath, a breath a moment.

I get lost in white hallways, supermarkets mainly,
lost in baked air, shelves half-gone
a cereal box tower I mistake for a shadow, an
arm.

When flashback is a breath and a breath a moment:
a dramatic day by the lake hits you
hits you again; this goes on.

I get lost in white hallways, libraries usually,
reading disrupted by the elevator bell:
a comforting sound where I thought there'd be
none.

When flashback is a breath, a breath a moment,
 everything is dream talk: ineffective,
a memory of a boat altered by my surfacing of it.

It's not breaths we count, but the gaps between
breaths,

my love, we just miss you so much –
lost in white hallways, the stairwell's sharp turn
when flashback is a breath, and the moment,
bombed sun, gone.
(**Theresa Muñoz**)

white hallways: violet doors

i-i slip away in pale doorways to paint violet
ellipses
an aperture in furniture for bodies unfolding
make future spaces where lips lisp in adjacence

i-i slip away in pale doorways to part violent
ellipses
slipping the breezes the bruises half-gone
or is it a love-bite there on my arm

marks a future space where lips lisp in adjacence
a fresh day at the beach issues a morning
still in you still for you looking to sea

i-i slip away in pale doorways to plant violets
ellipses
between notes barely half written down
while reading like breathing takes me on

makes space a future where lips lisp in adjacence

there are fins far out in these oceans
waiting for shaping ready to play

far out in these oceans there are fins
ready shaping our waiting to play
i-i slip away in pale doorways to paint violet
ellipses
mark future spaces where lips lisp in adjacence
(**Jane Goldman**)

SIX: Lynn Davidson and Jane Goldman:

[UNTITLED]

1.

My country is a piece of skin.
Frayed sleeve clouds.
Seagrass bending and lifting.
Warm slings of sand.

2.

My country is light across sashes.
Daily updates from the universe.
Dancing with the stars.
Dancing by myself.

3.

My country is a piece
Of frayed sleeve.
My country is
Yourself dancing.

4.

My country is an early thought.
I take it for a single walk.
Then take it home again.
For safety. It is a small brown bird.
For safety, it is a small brown bird.

(Lynn Davidson)

no country woman

∧

i-i am a no country woman
loosely rooted but i-i flow

the world is my country anarchist
a glen of weeping

is there a more romantic
existence in one country

in one art or has art now lost
its mental charms there's no

peace in avoiding life carry
me across any country under

ground for one country is two
systems what can poetry do

∧ ∧

what kind of utterances
damage civic space if speech

is the surplus of the kiss

in troubador country i-i

distrust landscape there's
instability in the countryside

these are phrases on an old
lady's purse destabilise this

text with the delicacy
and perfection

of its details see countryside
with detachment there's

always a polarising armory
show and lovers at the same

table with creme fraiche
keep it in your lap as you

enter the country of words
                    (**Jane Goldman**)

Gaar Adams
EC Lewis

The New Pantheon

I.

Sometime in the mid-18th century, a Glaswegian named Robert Wilson sailed down the Firth of Clyde and clear out into the Atlantic.[1]

It's safe to say that economic circumstances weighed heavily on Wilson in deciding to leave Glasgow for a new life—a new world—just as they would most Scots emigrating after the Jacobite rising of 1745. If he were a Presbyterian or Covenanter, then religion, of course, may also have played a factor.[2]

---

[1] I would consult the ship manifest for more specifics, but the definitive record I'm looking for, *Ships from Scotland to America, 1628-1828*, costs £27.50, and I put down a rental deposit on a converted West End tenement outside my means last autumn in a moment of weakness.

[2] Though it may seem ahistorical to consider an existential crisis, I do sometimes wonder if the looming religious fervor of the time sometimes masked or even obfuscated a deeper kind of anxiety, or even despair? Not even just in those who signed the National Covenant in 1638, necessarily, but anyone, really. My Glasgow flat is very expensive (original mouldings!) and sometimes when I hear those bells from St. Mary's reverberate across Great Western, even this atheist gets a little clammy and starts to wonder what in the hell he's doing here.

We do know that, somewhere in the Thirteen Colonies,[3] he had a son.[4] And his son had a son.[5,6] And that this second-generation American boy was named Samuel Wilson.

But you might know him better as Uncle Sam.[7]

───────────

[3] Probably Delaware, really whichever of the original Thirteen Colonies sounds like the most patriotic.

[4] Yes, the story of another dead white guy having a son. Yes, you've heard this one before.

[5] Full disclosure, also a white guy here. My father can trace our family back to a minor player of the Scottish Enlightenment, an engineer who had something to do with the invention of some kind of building material. My grandfather started a petition to get a wing of the new University of Glasgow Govan campus building named after him but was outbid by the family of a notable abolitionist.

[6] Did anyone have daughters? ....Maybe? Honestly, I could probably research a bit harder but it's not exactly central to the story here, and I have to finish this up pretty fast and write something that pays a bit better. Really not all about having to move back east to Barlanark again. Do *you* know what it's like having to explain to delivery guys that your place isn't the car wash or the tyre shoppe but the flat wedged between them??

[7] I'm not terribly used to—and, to be honest, don't have much patience for—those who don't get my Americentric historical references, so I'll wait here until you Google "Uncle Sam" so that it has the intended dramatic effect: Uncle Sam, a real man, the myth come to life.

II.

Just after arriving in Glasgow, I called my father in Illinois to pull out our family records. The Scottish inventor, James Duncan, the man we can trace back furthest on my paternal side was born in a little farmhouse out in what's now Drumchapel. I must admit: I haven't actually been. I heard a story about a friend of a friend who got a bottle thrown at him by some kid in broad daylight, so I've always steered clear.

Duncan worked in the quarries dotting the outskirts of Glasgow in the late 18th century before enrolling in an engineering program at the University in 1776, the year America clawed their way toward independence. After he graduated, he couldn't find a job, so he jumped on a boat and headed for the newly emerging United States. My dad says the family lore is that this was a common occurrence at the time, a kind of Great Scottish Brain Drain: you get smart, you can't find a job in a depressed economy, and so you skip town.

Duncan settled in Kentucky like a lot of the Scots at the time and, because of everything he learned in the mines, he messed around with sandstone and hydraulic lime until—no shit—he invented modern concrete. I did really wonder why the uni hadn't named some stuff after him.

A bunch of his descendants held notable professions in Kentucky and the surrounding states. Some were well-known preachers; some were lawyers; some were even entrepreneurs and inventors, taking after the patriarch who started it all. One of my relatives—my great-great-great granduncle—even began a farming company that now manufactures America's leading potato cultivation equipment.

He said he would send the rest of his typewritten copy when he could get around to a photocopier, but I know how he is with technology, so I scribbled as much as I could over our call:

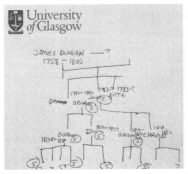

I took notes so quickly that my hand cramped; I almost forgot to ask why I kept having to write and circle the letter "S" next to so many of the names. For a moment, the line went silent.

"With a typewriter, the word 'slave-owner' takes up too much space on the page," he said. Then he hung up.

III.

I

make
religion,   free
                                              of
                                          people
                    and
                        grievances.

II
                                        the
                                    people
                    shall   be infringed.
III
No   time of peace   in
any house,   the consent
        of war,

IV
                be secure in
        papers,
                                not
violated,
                by Oath

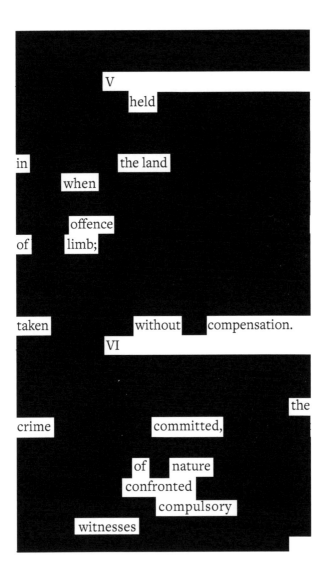

V

held

in   the land

when

offence

of   limb;

taken   without   compensation.

VI

the

crime   committed,

of   nature

confronted

compulsory

witnesses

VII

no
re-examined

rules

VIII

required,

imposed,   cruel

IX

enumeration

to deny

others

X

powers

prohibited

are reserved

XI

construed   in
equity,   prosecuted against
                                another

XII

distinct

lists

I

number

and certify, and transmit

to

all

the   counted; --

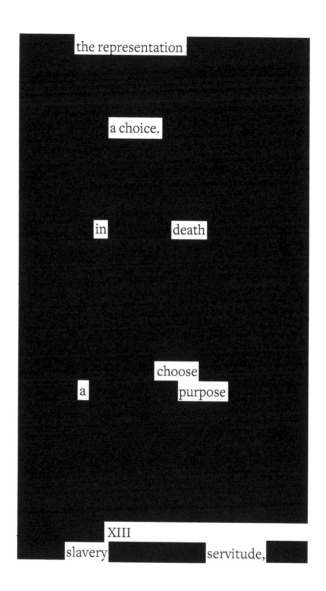

the representation

a choice.

in   death

choose
a   purpose

XIII
slavery   servitude,

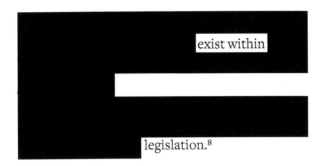

exist within

legislation.[8]

8 "All Amendments to the United States Constitution." All Amendments to the United States Constitution. University of Michigan: Human Rights Library. Accessed May 15, 2020. http://hrlibrary.umn.edu/education/all_amendments_usconst. htm.

IV.

I certainly had intended to know more specifics about my family history before that phone call. After all, I decided to live halfway around the world in Glasgow in order to find some kind of connection with my Scottish heritage. I came to get my master's in engineering, yes, but I suppose I thought that by studying on the same campus and walking the same Govanhill streets as the Duncan who started it all, I might also find—I don't really even know now—perhaps a fragment of myself glinting back at me in the Clyde?

A few months after I arrived, I sat with a couple of Glaswegian friends on a rickety bench outside Jinty McGintys. I loved that mound in the back of the pub—you could look down all of Ashton Lane from that little patio, but to me, it felt like I could see the whole city. We had plans to go on a hillwalk around Campie Glen that morning, but we had all woken up so hungover that we instead opted for paracetamol and breakfast at The Chip. If we were feeling better by then, perhaps there would be time to catch the train to Dumbarton Castle. It was one of those days no one had told me about before I arrived in Glasgow—the sun shining with such a ferocity that it makes you squint. I didn't even own a pair of sunglasses. We ended up back at Jintys instead—or, rather, again—my pint of Guinness warm before I even sat down.

A few drinks in, we were swapping family stories and I started in on one about picking up the phone when I was about eight years old to hear a strange voice asking to speak with my father. He said he was my dad's cousin—or second cousin, or great-uncle, I don't really remember now—calling from Kentucky to wish my old man a happy birthday. It must have been the first time we had spoken. We exchanged a few pleasantries, but his Southern accent was so thick that I could barely make out what he was saying; he drew out his vowels in places that took my ear by surprise. Before I passed the phone over to my father, I remember him saying, "Damn, boy, you sure do sound like a Yankee!"

The story didn't land with the kind of weight I thought it would. Or, at least, the weight I thought, at the time, it should. I think I tried to explain about my Scottish relatives landing in Kentucky, spreading out across the States over the centuries. About the Civil War, the Reformation. I couldn't tell if I hadn't told the story right or they didn't understand the history. But perhaps it was just that I had one too many pints.

I don't remember how I even got back to my flat in Barlanark, though I've had plenty of nights like that. Past the fairy lights of Ashton Lane, past the man camped outside Iceland selling The Big Issue, past the sandstone tenements built from the quarries in my family lore. I was sure I knew it all, my new home.

V.

Two generations removed from Scotland, the real Uncle Sam was born in Arlington,[9] Massachusetts.[10] He joined the Continental Army at fourteen[11] and then traveled a hundred miles west on foot through the Green Mountains[12] until the Hudson met the shining Mohawk River in what's now Troy, New York.

After he arrived in New York,[13][14] Samuel Wilson built a business constructing the first American-made bricks,[15] a success he parlayed into establishing a slaughterhouse with his brother, Ebenezer. It was this burgeoning

---

[9] Name changed from the original Algonquian to preserve white fragility.

[10] The Commonwealth of Massachusetts did preserve the name of the indiginous population, but its flag also depicts a white colonist holding a sword over a Native American and the Latin motto "By the sword we seek peace, but peace only under liberty". So I guess it's kind of a wash?

[11] Seems a little young? Indoctrination, normalization of war, etc.

[12] Why hasn't this been made into a film yet?! Hollywood loves a white male origin story depicting struggle.

[13] "Start spreadin' the news, I'm leavin' today/I want to be a part of it/New York, New York/These vagabond shoes, are longing to stray/Right through the very heart of it/New York, New York"

[14] "Concrete jungle where dreams are made of/There's nothing you can't do/Now you're in New York/ These streets will make you feel brand new/Big lights will inspire you/Hear it for New York, New York, New York"

[15] Previously, most had been imported from the Netherlands, and we all know how we Americans like to fetishize that which is Made In America. I mean, just Google "Freedom Fries". I'll wait.

American meat empire,[16] E & S Wilson, that secured a contract to supply American armed services in the Greenbush, New York, area with food for an entire calendar year.

Alongside the company name, these 5,000 wooden barrels of beef and pork were also emblazoned with "U.S" stamps to denote its American origin. But enlistees, many from Troy, conflated these initials with those of Uncle Sam, by then a beloved figure who was also meat inspector for the entire Union Army. Servicemen across the country began referring to all government possessions stamped "U.S." as property of Uncle Sam; he was even memorialized in one of America's patriotic songs[17] Yankee Doodle.[18]

Over time, Samuel Wilson, the grandson of an immigrant boy from Glasgow, the pride of Troy, came to represent[19] the entire United States.

---

16 After the Hollywood film is inevitably made, might I suggest some patriotic tie-in merchandise like a LEGO® playset or at least a Disney theme park ride called "Burgeoning American Meat Empire"? It will surely make millions.

17 We have many.

18 Old Uncle Sam came there to change/Some pancakes & some onions/ For lasses cakes to carry home/To give his wife & young ones

19 Symbolize? Personify? Embody? Engulf?

VI.

cried,   aloud

wretched   fury

What   possess'd

you

foes;

above

and

by   force:

Trust   horse

His   hissing

yielding

And trembling

a rattling sound,

And groans

the wound

not

fated to be

Enough

Then

with shouts,

in bands,

Taken to take;   their prey,

their belief,

bent

undaunted,

All   to see,

Now hear

a nation

Trembling   and

bound

[20]

20 Dryden, John, trans. "The Internet Classics Archive: The Aeneid by Virgil." The Internet Classics Archive | The Aeneid by Virgil. Accessed May 15, 2020. http://classics.mit.edu/Virgil/aeneid.2.ii.html.

VII.

Sometime in the mid-12th century BC, a Trojan named Aeneas sailed past Tenedos and clear out into the Ionian.[21]

In *The Aeneid*, Virgil[22] tells the story of Aeneas's quest to establish a new home for his displaced countrymen after their defeat[23] at the hands of the Greeks in the Trojan War. With their steadfast leader at the helm, the Trojans set off in search of a new life—a new world—across the sea.[24]

The reestablishment of Troy is entwined with Aeneas's fate; as the epic unfolds, the two are so inextricably linked that Aeneas undermines his own happiness and sacrifices his own personality to recreate his city. He is a man,[25] a warrior, the quintessential patriarchal figure bound by duty

---

21 I would consult the ship manifest, but Aeneas is most likely a mythological figure. Though, in school, we were taught that about Uncle Sam, too.

22 Fun fact, Virgil also means 'staff bearer.' This may seem like useless information, but call me when this is the bonus question during the final round of a pub quiz.

23 A more historically accurate wording for this might be slaughter but hey ho, there you go.

24 Terms and conditions apply. Not valid for those already living in Italy.

25 Yes, the story of another dead white guy having a son; yes, you've heard this one before.

and celebrated for his altruistic concern for the collective.[26]

The city of Troy, New York, once held another name entirely.[27] It was not until the year Samuel Wilson arrived on foot that it was renamed.[28] Later, it took its motto "Ilium fuit, Troja est" (Troy was, Troy is) from a line in The Aeneid. A town named something once again became Troy: a city destroyed and reborn[29] across both mythology and history untold[30] times.

When Wilson's first Troy-based businesses began to take off, he was declared Path Master of the city. It was a title that today might be akin to Road Commissioner but sounds like so much more, as though it were only Uncle Sam who could show the way.

---

26 I can't keep writing "Terms and conditions apply." I'll surely run out of room to note them all.

27 Not central to this story. Look it up on your own time. Victors dominate history. Conquerors tell stories.

28 When my family's petition to name a wing of a University of Glasgow building after my James Duncan was denied, we got a small mound at the outskirts of our Illinois town named after him. It already had a native Algonquian name, but no one left in town could remember it.

29 Tourism brochures say it has a wealth of Victorian architecture!

30 VICTORS DOMINANT HISTORY. CONQUERORS TELL STORIES.

VIII.

I only wanted to only take Engineering courses, but I'm required by the uni to take one elective so I'm in this American history class, mostly because I thought it would be easy. I thought I would be able to dissect it all from a distance. The class is in a different building to where I'm used to being, but it looks like all the others. I wanted so badly for everything in Glasgow to be new, always new, but I just keep circling these same campus blocks.

I was late on the first day because the faucet in my new flat didn't work and I missed the guy who worked in the tyre shoppe next to my old flat in Barlanark because I know he could have fixed it.

When I entered the room, a political cartoon of Uncle Sam was projected on the screen. We got through a whole class without talking about him being Scottish. I couldn't believe it. I thought a hundred times about raising my hand but didn't. What would I say? That over three hundred years ago, a grandfather fled a war for his grandson to feed servicemen in another war? That Wilson would feed a war with barrels of meat just like Uncle Sam did with barrels of propaganda? Greenock, Scotland, would become Greenbush, New York in under a hundred years, just like how Wilson could walk from one city to another a hundred miles. Was I supposed to interject that a nameless town in a new world could become Troy, and Troy could become nothing? That you could escape one empire only to build a new one?

Where would I start, with Wilson fleeing Glasgow just like how Aeneas fled Troy? Or that I fled a new world for the old world which was really the new one, but just for me?

That this is all just a mythology created within a closed circle of white men whose stories we hear again and again but never really listen for a moral because if we did we would be somehow admitting that what they did wasn't really that bad. We don't really study history. We don't read literature. We just watch the movie Troy filmed in a Hollywood studio, and violence just begets more violence. The Trojans kicked out by the Greeks, the Trojans colonizing the Italians, the Scots kicked out by Jacobite Rising, the Scots becoming the Americans, the Americans colonizing everyone and the war and the slaves and on and on and on.

If I started talking, I'd start somewhere factual like how thirty-five out of forty-five American presidents have Scottish blood, but I'd end up somewhere absurd like how some of those are Ulster Scot, and I don't really know what that means because only conquerors tell stories. Aeneas isn't a hero but a colonizer and mythology is prop-aganda is Samuel Wilson is Uncle Sam is a war-monger is

America is me.

I'd want to know if all my Scottish family had already fled the highlands and the lowlands and left Glasgow an empty city for no one to explore but me, then what would it mean if I thought I knew every street, every cobblestone before I even arrived? I'd want to ask if my family tree was empty or broken, except it's not at all—I can trace back to a man who studied in these same damn halls and they are mine, the whole city is mine, the whole world is mine.

Your country doesn't need you. Ask not what you can do for your country because you are your country and your country is you are Uncle Sam I am. Flee your own land to destroy another's. Make it your own and then give contracts to other men who look like you to make more war.

I came here to study engineering, to create something like that man my father and his father and his father before him used to tell stories and facts and myths about. Now I study my own innocence and all I create are circles and circles and erasure marks that tear holes through perfectly good pages.

IX.

The

centuries   received   and
                              benefitted
from   such
gifts

                many

                petitioned

                              recognition

                in so doing,

                              barred from doing so

instructed
and   prepared

then formed

At the same

the   consortium

nature

accrued

as a result

possible acts of

justice

reparative

ideals of truth

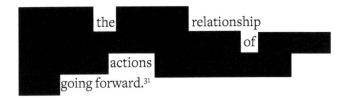

the relationship of actions going forward.[31]

---

31 Mullen, Stephen, and Simon Newman. "University of Glasgow Slavery Studies." University of Glasgow, September 2018. https://www.gla.ac.uk/media/Media_607547_smxx.pdf.

Esther Draycott
Gwen Dupré
Kiah Endelman Music

SKIRTS

I would get these body tremors, I still get them sometimes. I wake thinking that someone is outside drilling but it is just my body shaking and I cannot control it or even locate its source.

Nick Hedges, *A Life Worth Living*, 1971.

In half-light, an image of children playing in the back court of the crowded tenement, or of women walking down the road lined with empty factories, windows shattered, lies somewhere between history and memory. The past finds a fixed location in these long streets—how things were is both recovered and laid to rest. Complexity of thought, past desires, wants and distinctions, are foreclosed by the meagre material of subjects' surroundings. A sense of loss is inherent both to the construction of the image and mechanisms of its interpretation. She has been captured.

—

*To play truant from work and visit The Hideout before Friday
and ask to see the wicked album will be admitting a sexual need.
June has never in her life admitted a sexual need to another adult.
She waits till Friday before returning to The Hideout, and forces
herself to wait till mid-afternoon, instead of arriving like an eager
little girl as soon as it opens.*

*And she stands on the cracked pavement between the loan office
and the betting shop and stares at a space of reddish, brick-strewn
gravel with a railway viaduct behind it. For a while she cannot
believe the whole building has vanished. She fights the desolate
frustration she feels by examining the rows of buildings on each
side of the space, and going into a pub across the road from it,
though it is the sort of pub where lonely women are stared at. She
orders a gin and tonic and asks the barman, "What happened to
the tailoring business across the road?"*

"Those shops were pulled down weeks ago."

"Oh no – they were there last Friday."

"Could be. But nobody's been in them for years."

"But there was a ... a leathercraft shop upstairs in one. Called The Hideout. A small woman ran it. She advertised with a sign on a parked car."
"She couldn't have. Parking's illegal on that side."

June finishes her drink then goes to the fashionable leatherwear shop which gave her the address. The only information the assistant has is a card a stranger handed in with The Hideout's name and address on it.

She says, "These small firms come and go very quickly. Will I give you the address of another?"

She often feels to be put upon by an object – not unkind but remainders of encounter with the world. With a longing to a memory, as the hem of her skirt begins its fall back down, hers is a want to give herself up, to make herself sensational.

And here above her head she heaves her skirt caught tight between her hands with nails dug hard in part in the pulling fabric now and also into her skin. Over her head, her eyes, she'd not be able to see (under), nor be seen either – anyway

Her footing slips and catches itself.

—

In a 1986 public interview at the ICA, Kathy Acker asks Alasdair Gray: *Have you ever worked with a woman as a main character?*

Only in some plays, he answers, but always she's been seen in relation to a man. I haven't the insight to imagine how a woman is to herself.

your body lofty stone
catching my rising panic

Raphael Samuels described the thrill evoked by the close study of period photography as *scopophilia*: a desire to see. Black-and-white studies of old Gorbals evoke a deceptive flash of recognition.[1] In the photograph one sees a former version of oneself, no matter the subject, and feels sadness for the loss of it. These are the *impossible longings and regressive fantasies* of returning somewhere you have never been.[2]

A baby sleeps under a pile of rags while a mother and daughter sit at a cluttered table. Among the objects in front of them: a knife, a spoon, a butter dish and a salt shaker. Each has a thin gleam—a sign of repeated use. Picked out by an adjacent window, the photograph may otherwise catch the brief glint off the blurred frame of a mirror, a bracelet catching on a loose thread, or the rim of a vase on a bedroom dresser. These coats of light belong to the daughter, the mother, and the mothers before them: their gathered heat.[3]

As the photographer's lens captures light over small objects in the crowded room, they attain the sensual

[1] Bert Hardy, *Gorbals, 1948*, a documentary photo series in Picture Post, many of which were later reproduced as greetings cards and framed prints, with two purchased by the National Gallery of Scotland.
[2] Raphael Samuels, *Theatres of Memory Volume 1*, first published by Verso in 1994 and republished in 2013 due to a spike in demand.
[3] Gaston Bachelard, *The Poetics of Space*, Beacon Press, 1957.

power afforded to the souvenir or miniature. Susan Stuart, *On Longing*: shrinking and displacing a figment of an authentic experience, to provide the illusion of committing the event itself to memory, addresses the mind's *insatiable demand* for a past vacated of impurity.

The tiny objects littering the photograph of the Gorbals dwelling are fetishes in which *part of the body, or object, is substituted for the whole body, or object*, resulting in the contradictory emotional sensations of loss—of the body or object's original meaning or value—with a surplus of feeling created by its smaller, glistening substitution.

the ship's prow
a finger down a spine

unbuckling a gate onto cut lawns or concrete. I prefer to
remain anonymous. I have incessant thoughts that every
abandoned building in this city is a sex club. Every knoll a
place for coupling.

following the rubble, the rain

—

In 2015, curator and writer Natasha Hoare interviewed Gray for *Extra Extra*, an erotic magazine exploring culture. She asks:

Legend has it that Kathy Acker encouraged you to write with a female protagonist and thus you wrote Something Leather?

He replies:

At an interview in London Kathy Acker asked why I had never written fiction from a woman's point of view. I said I did not know women enough to do so. Her question may have prompted me to attempt it in Something Leather.

An ankle glances hard again against the heel and cuts it always only minutes from the floor – she turns on empty shoulders ready to be caught.

Not expected and deliberate, these are moments of the dance. Not to avoid faulting as to feel her landing/show. Swaying, knows that she is seen. She has been running in the streets.

Watch: not unhurried but at will, she does not pace herself. Stunting, she will be a stand in, knows her/will not stay in place.[1]

There is possibility and this may be an error, bred/the making of desire.[2] She knows in practice not for prudence but for sense. She is riding high.

Her heels cut and sharp and striking, staggered on the ground, even steps are lost. She recollects, I want the glory of a fall.[3] It is not always even/easy motion for which she volunteers.

She takes in hand her skirt and pulls and there occurs a scene which bodies forth in an uneasy fashion this, the challenge posed by her, an object known as bad.[4]

Sees that these are fabrics made more so to drop than be allowed to fall. These are details to be missed. A sweeping generalisation: she should take better care.[5]

[1] In *The Female Grotesque*, Mary Russo describes what she calls 'stunting' as a tactical manoeuvre and critical practice of *provisional, uncomfortable, even conflictual coalitions of bodies which both respect the concept of situated knowledges and refuse to keep every body in its place. An embodiment of possibility and of error belonging to the improvisational, the realm of the possible.*

[2] Della Pollok, in her essay *The Performative "I"*, writes of Russo's 'stunting' that *where there is possibility there is error: the mistake, imperfection, or transgression that challenges the normative repetition of the same and so invites correction, punishment, and recrimination. The thrill of flight, for Russo, is heightened by the chance of falling, of getting things terribly wrong, by risking death or its semiotic correlate, abjection.*

[3] *Do I not have a plot to my life? I am piecemeal. My story is living. And I have no fear of failure. Let failure annihilate me. I want the glory of falling.* Clarice Lispector, *Água Viva*.

[4] In an essay of the same name, Naomi Schor writes of choosing 'bad objects' of study; specific sites deemed to be improper, unserious, of illicit character. She suggests it as a strategy of reading, a critical perversion; what she calls 'female fetishism'.

In a foreword to Schor's later book, *Reading in Detail*, Ellen Rooney expands on the aesthetics of the bad object, writing that *the branding of the bad object – as taboo, marginal, partial, particular, prosaic, in other words, as a species of detail – demands that we read it as a symptom, a compromise, a displacement, a supplement, indeed, as a fetish...The bad object is impure.*

[5] Schor writes of the detail's particularity as a *framing of the general*, that, *at moments of aesthetic mutation, the detail becomes a means not only of effecting change, but of understanding it.* She recognises the political and gendered history of the detail, suggesting that, rather than essentially feminine, the detail has been insistently understood as feminine – or, feminised. Detail itself is a 'bad object'.

each time, the journey towards you
a trip with purpose
falling against the shadow of repetition

the city worn as an outfit
objects about you moulding to form.

Smallness implies psychological simplicity.[1] The period photograph is composed of rows of toy tenements, winding stairwells, patchwork courts and narrow roads. Rubble, mulch, smoke and shit give the surface of the images a haptic quality—finely-textured layers that diminish the scene like gauze. Oscar Marzaroli, *Boys in High Heels*, 1963: three boys stand in an empty road on an old Gorbals street. One stands, hands clasped, looking on as the other two bend at a right angle. Each wears a pair of large black stilettos. Deprived of their original use and use-value, the shoes bring with them a dim imprint of the owner's taut calves, her tense spine, rounded hips shifting. 2008, buildings gone, a sculpture casts the image back to the ground on which the subjects stood. Shoes, this time detailed in silver, stripped and blinking.

Peggy Phelan: *To what end are we seeking an escape from bodies?*[2] Any recoverable element of a history of desire is bound to a recognition of its larger *irreparable loss*, the affective outline of a departure. Saidiya Hartman: *pangs of desire unsettle* the period photograph's captions (read: *A Life Worth Living*) and *hint at the possibility of a life bigger* than the field of vision it represents. In images depicting the faint

silhouette of her subject—a newspaper headline, an exhibit, a brief portrait—she cannot see but imagines, closely, small

[1] Carolyn Steedman, *Landscape for a Good Woman*, Virago, 1986.

[2] Peggy Phelan, *Mourning Sex: Performing Public Memories*, Routledge, 1997.

objects shaken of their duty to the present: *the cool slip of silk undergarments against her flesh, smooth and releasing all that fire.*[3]

---

[3] Saidiya Hartman, *Wayward Lives, Beautiful Experiments*, Serpent's Tail, 2019.

Alternatively you may think of her towering body. Taut and upright as it balances on a pair of high heels, walking across the city, it disappears from view.

Taken off she could hold heel in hand, cupped
and running over – reading for some proof.
She would sense a disappointment as a mark/a nick/a
character would fade. To stay (still) would be to
indicate an action made to fail.

Greg Thomas
Saskia McCracken

The rocking horse and others

Loved living in _____
Mum, Dad, Irish immigrant
community
music, culture
then _____ &
restaurants
&

_____, a great shopping centre
Woolworths _____ & Looking Glass
_____ Van on a Thursday
making ice cream
float on a Sunday

All the shops down the whole of _____
Rd & round the corner of _____ Rd
the buzz of the place

At one time plenty of shops
now very little shops
in area – parks
good but neglected

"In the 40s Govanhill was a destination place to buy for young couples"
Folks moved out of _____

Mum traveling from _____ to _____
Road to do shopping
rather than going into town
bakers, pubs, hardware shops

My aunt's gas lamp above her range cooker
someone used to come and light the
close lamps
in the _____

The _____ Tavern
by the _____
at _____. One of Glasgow's
very last windowless pubs
live music
a rare tucked
away scheme pub

1941
parents moved into a room with outside toilet
3 stairs up in _____
9 months later dad went round
to stay the night at his parents
round the corner

at _____ Ave.
Next day he met the district nurse
'You have a son'
Very nice
he said

Year later
took his son to stay
the night with his parents again
Going home the next day the district nurse says
'you have a daughter'
Very nice
dad says

Year later same scenario
Meets the district nurse
'You have a son'
Good
he says
Then she says 'you have a daughter'
'Och make your mind up' 'Oh yes' she says

'Twins'

My mother was so worried
about how they would manage

Born on _____ Rd
played (2-4 years)
in the back dunnie
coal bunker up the close and outside toilet

Waiting to get into _____ baths
children grinding pennies
into the sandstone
see the round marks
still

The _____ Garden Festival
first roller coaster
music noise atmosphere

Special times on the _____ 1970-77
sailing from Glasgow & Dunoon
to all corners
on board as it left _____ pier
so silent and smooth with steam turbines
only realised it was moving
when I looked out of the window

'What would you like me to do today'
 (first day on job)
'well here's a sledge hammer
– go and demolish the gents toilets'
 Certainly

Grew up in _____ St.
The only car belonged to an Elder
in the Church of Scotland
Went to the baths
tennis in _____ Park
books from the library

Every Saturday
morning ponies
brought to
_____ Park
up _____ Road
from stables in _____
Great memories
of riding the pony

Rolling Easter
eggs in the park

All kinds of shops
haberdashery, shoe shops, bakers etc
The tailor's
at _____ Street
tailor sat cross-legged
in the window

Women stayed at home
had to get their messages (groceries)

on a daily basis
so the shops of _____
were crucial

Spent hours in _____ Hall
all the time as kids
doing religious
groups
singing kids
club & things
I'd love
to go back

Hoping on free buses
to the _____ family day
event at _____ Park
The free buses
were part of the whole
day experience
very much appreciated

****

climbing dykes

in the backcourts

playing in the garden
 less cars

Disco tower
blocks ***

trolley carts

getting hugely invested
in the swans

white skating
skirts

the winter of ___
one of the coldest ever recorded.
Everything was frozen.
For weeks the world was glittering white
with huge spangled drifts of snow
lying in the folds of the hills around Pollokshaws
Almost nothing moved in the silence
except the draughty old trams
that took us to school in town

My family moved in ___, it was a lovely place then, all fields
& trees with the burn, where we all gathered to watch the
gypsies, with their beautiful coloured caravans, we also had
guides and girls training courses in those days there was
plenty put on in schools to keep young ones busy at [illegible]
and bus [illegible] at weekend and a matinees on Saturday

Since the 5 years ago
the people of _____ and _____ have treat me like [illegible]
more
one of them
and helped and given me the opportunities to find my place
New to the country
Thanks to you all!!
[illegible]

Went with Mum to register for school –
there was a rocking horse outside the classroom
had a great time on it
waiting for the teacher to call our name

was so excited to start school after the summer
when the day arrived I was so sad
no rocking horse
never saw it again.

[Based on selected fragments from the "Southside Memories Postcard Project" (Autumn 2019). Memories anonymously posted by south Glasgow residents and reproduced courtesy of South Glasgow Heritage and Environment Trust. With thanks to the authors.]

K Patrick
Adrien H. Howard

There is a building in the city centre which looks different to a lot of others. It opened   as The Beresford hotel sometime in the 1930's and then repurposed into a number of privately owned residences sometime after that. The style falls somewhere between art deco and something called 'streamline moderne' which is a name I like a lot. When someone says the word 'streamline', I think about design features whose purpose is for ease of movement and so for a building which is predominantly static, I find it oddly funny. When walking by I cross the street to get a better view, craning my neck and letting my mouth hang open as I look up. Small single-glazed windows sit in perfect alignment on the facade. Two smooth, round columns with windows reaching around. The glass is old so it is beginning to drop and sag. Causing ripples and waves in the outside world. I think about looking at the city like that, through the droop. How it distorts the view.

I'm writing this from memory now and you can tell. Both things are real, the memory and the building, just one in a less bricks and mortar for all to see kind of way.

A friend used to live in it, the building, not my memory. She told me once or twice but I never followed her up on it. Perhaps I didn't want the two things to become confused.

The pale stucco and rounded shapes of the architecture remind me of my body or maybe that's the other way around. Now, how my spine curves as I twist to see my back in the mirror.

Limbs straight and long. This is a different kind of architecture, a different kind of house. My body is more fleshy, it has blood running through. It runs hot and cold, it is changing and growing old. These two different architectures have those things in common.

You and I talk about that often: buildings and repurposing bodies.

I look across and I can see your window. We wave to one another sometimes. I often think I can hear your voice or the dog bark, but it could be anyone or anybody's dog. I take pleasure in these absent communications now. In the evening when I am making something to eat I look across and I can see small cracks of light from around the edges of the curtain, where it fails to meet the wall. The light in the room means there is something happening, it's off and it's the end of the day for you, resting limbs, shallow breaths, eyes closed. I'll see you again tomorrow, from behind the curtain.

The Finnieston Crane is so broad-shouldered. I've acquired this lazy habit in which I categorise great moments of engineering as butch. Butch is not a sentiment but a body. Barely even a word, there's no history in it. Quick efficiency of a motorway, the airless meeting of rubber and tarmac. Powerful knees of a bridge. Muscular tension of any cable. There is cunt in cantilever. Slow, precise movements. Smell of warm metal on your fingers, punched blood. Steam-bent bone. Only a butch could harness the river, make the most of its sway. Wetness, too. The buttress of a dam. Knuckles. In butch there is something left behind. Place the puffed out chest over the old steel skeleton. Leave the light chaotic across the bedspread. An industry never tires of its city.

Apparently this is a myth, that glass sags over time. At least, it does not change its shape in a time relevant to humans. Perhaps in strange-time it does. Glass behaves like liquid at times and so I suppose I thought it sagged due to the effect of gravity. I'm told that windows are made by floating molten glass on a bed of molten tin, naturally this is called the 'float method'. Before that the glass for a window was cut from blown cylinders or disks which is then quickly flattened. This causes the glass to be thicker at the bottom than it is at the top. This is what causes the distortion.

The last time we walked together it was through the center of the city. We reached the street where the building stood to find a thin layer of molten glass across the pavement. Hot, the soles of shoes became tacky as the rubber began to melt. Glass only liquifies when it reaches a temperature somewhere between 1400 and 1600 degrees celsius.

We both looked up to see that the building was spilling its windows. The panes had softened and were sliding from their frames, down the exterior walls and onto the hard concrete below. The building now stands with perforated walls which the air passes freely through. This is a time relevant to ghosts.

Two wasps are living behind my knees. I think the wasps are male because they have not stung me yet. Only female wasps have stingers, which are actually 'modified egg-laying organs'. I found this out when looking online for humane ways to get rid of them. Someone suggested sleeping next to an open jar of jam but I cannot stand the smell of strawberries. In my dreams there are wasps unbuttoning their shirts, lifting their skirts. For the past few nights I have sweated through my sheets. Not because of the heat, but in anticipation of it. The wasps did not like this, growling at me each time I crawled to the bathroom to rinse my face. Salt crusted on my eyelashes, knuckles stuck together. I am worried more wasps will come if I don't treat them well. A wasp in distress releases a pheromone that requests violent assistance from the nearest hive. Gagging, I stick my fingers into the jar and wipe jam across the backs of my thighs. Hum gently to them in the dark. This seems to work: I feel their purring in the folds of my skin.

We're only moving between two or three places: our flats, the nearest parks, supermarkets where we feel safest. You have a car and drive to Morrisons. I've done Lidl once, but otherwise stick to the small shop up the road. Each morning I eat an innocent breakfast of eggs.

Everyone is already talking about going swimming. At the borders of Pollok Park there is a neat river, once channelled into a water mill. Old pottery and smooth glass in the slow-moving water. A growing collection of fragments on the grassy banks. The neck of a Heineken beer bottle alongside the shard of a blue and white plate. I don't know what to wear to go swimming. We've talked about this: I prefer to be folded in two. Why are there so many reflective surfaces? A tree dips its branches into the river, cracking the mirror. I've been thinking about all the books on wild swimming and city swimming. There are too many of them. I'll just say it: people shouldn't take so much pleasure in swimming. Bodies don't belong in water! Have you ever seen an elbow?! Summer is embarrassing. Especially when burgeoning. Not unlike poetry, which is something we have both agreed on.

In the deeper section of Pollok Park there is a tree with SEX carved into the trunk. You tell me that this graffiti is at least one hundred years old. Here is strange-time, come to us. Moss grows across the curves of the S. Bark split like lips around the X. The E carries finer, toothier impressions showing the work of whatever tool was used: the flat edge of a chisel, maybe tapped with a hammer. I like to imagine the powerful, small blows, the maker's neck straining up at the canopy, eyes sensitive with leaves and light, shoulder firm against the trunk, hands smoothing over the bark, miming the carving about to take place, practicing, thinking through the shape of each letter, the individual intricacies: the E's pragmatism and handlebars, the fast erotics of an S, the surreality of X . In a word like sex, each letter has a chance. There are only a few words like this. Fewer carved into a tree. The sound of each letter, each blow of chisel, still echoing a century later. Above the large, confident SEX a first attempt is also visible: a smaller, more cautious 'sex'. Spelled out in lower case, the letters gone faint with time. SEX tree is Glasgow: a posh park slightly undone, a quick joke made slow.

The alphabet is a strange-place, full of
strange-time. Like an octopus, it has a
decentralised nervous system. A small brain in
every tentacle. Each component part of a
whole, and yet able to think and feel on its
own terms.

(Ghosts love initials, for example. This is
the trace left behind: the fastest spelling on a
ouija board, the marks left on trees, on
a cotton nightdress, on flesh. Ghosts don't
have time for words. Ghosts don't have
time. Only letters will do, and only out of
vague respect for the living.)

**(I've already warned you about the wasps but
I'll say it again: tape A4 paper to the vents in
your flat, use a knife to cut narrow slits, press
your ear to the wall, (the noise is not obvious
at first, a breeze chasing a breeze, your earlobe
turning hot) when you hear the wasps coming
put your mouth to a slit and blow softly.)**

Retreat retreat retreat.

Spring used to be so full of itself. Blue sky bouncing along, clouds imitating breath, flowers flushing your cheeks, faint cackling of leaves. I swear the daffodils are cancelled earlier each year. Have you noticed? (I feel bad for saying that about Spring. Who knows how much longer it will be around.) The cherry blossom tree outside my window is desperate with petals. They cling to everything. Each evening I listen as my neighbour beats the welcome mat, sweeps the concrete floors. She tips the petals into the bin. I see them when I take out my rubbish, stuck to the plastic edges like tiny, wet tongues. Brown veins thickening through the light pink. I don't have the stomach to scrape them off.

On Tuesday I water the flowers in
the garden, the one I share with my
neighbours. Holding tightly to one end
I drag a long stretch of hose pipe from
the tap at the back of the building across
the carpark to the grass. It is spring and
the hydrangea has flowered. The petals
are such a deep blue. You can encour-
age hydrangia to grow different colours
depending on the ph. of the soil. They
grow blue in soil which is more acidic.
These are a much deeper and more vivid
than I have seen before. A blue so full
and brimming that the colour spills and
stains the grass. If the colour is deep
enough you can descend into it, making
sure you hold tightly to the hosepipe.
It is the line back to the surface.

I'm walking alone late in the evening along the streets close to where we both live. As I turn the corner (the one which takes me back home) there is a couple standing in the street light about 10 meters in front of me. It's late and these are the first people I have seen. I am taken aback. I stand for a second and watch in the shadow as the conversation looks fraught. I can hear the air leaving their mouths quickly. Acute whisps. Sharp words. I stand still, not wanting to interrupt. I even hold my breath. Two foxes also watch from the other side of the road. They notice me too. All three of us poised here as if independent adjudicators to the couples dispute.

Yesterday whilst walking the dog a group of four teenage boys cycled past me. Unprovoked, one of them yelled 'FAGGOT'. An insult intended for me. This prompted three pubescent laughs from the other boys and for my small dog to bark furiously. (as if in defence of my mannerisms and tendencies.)

It's been a number of weeks since I've interacted with strangers. I'm glad this was the first time.
They were more right than they would ever know.

Like 'sex', 'faggot' is also a word where every letter is given a chance.

I can't tell what if I'm remembering a dream or if its a memory from a time of being awake.

In the morning mornings I am woken up by the the gulls which cry out as if somebody has set their wings on fire. I sit up in bed and see the two foxes again, this time watching from

the foot of the bed.

I have seen the same foxes as you. Waiting for something, side by side. They move from the hedge in front of my flat, cross St Johns Road and sit in front of your building. Both of our mid-century   flats are located within the walls of old estates. We are always penned in by a 'before'. Plenty of things look better in the dark, but foxes especially. I'd love to inhale my own shadow. Cold on my tongue, my sensitive teeth. My dog is furious at the idea. She whines impatiently at the window, their smell lifted into moonlight, into sleepy pollen, into pieces of stiffened breeze.

Confined to her room with an illness, the Polish artist Maria
Pinińska-Bereś wrote 'a window view is not the real thing'
You call me while standing on your balcony, waving. I stand
in the lounge, holding my phone to my ear until we realise
that our voices are able to carry across. Now we disturb the
neighbours and the smaller birds. St Johns Road is between
us. It's a long, elegant slope. These days kids speed down on
their bikes, or skateboards, or scooters. Helmets unnatural,
slipping down their foreheads.

I can't think beyond a dandelion. On a government-issued walk I see a whole clump of them, ripped out of the ground and discarded on the hot pavement. The neighbourhood is wealthy. Two hundred year old stained glass is expensively preserved in each house I go past. Yellow petals turned to wispy florets. Dandelions have a variety of ancient nicknames, including 'clockface'. I trust you with this information: when snapped, the stem secretes a latex. As kids we blew gently, hoping to tell the time from the remaining puffy seeds. Now I feel more violent towards the present tense. By design, the dandelion encourages this. The harder I blow on the face, the more I empty the clock, the better the chance of pollination. The dandelion is satisfied. I can justify my violence. I would call this strange-time. Plants move and I am undone.

You and I both suffer from hayfever. This does not surprise me. The outside drifting in, inflaming the edges of the body. Eyes milky and full of grit.

What about the rhododendrons? In Glasgow they make the parks especially aesthetically pleasing. But many scientists have labelled them a 'complex variable hybrid swarm' or 'monsters' for short. The Victorians wanted the purple, red and pink flowers to cover their estates, providing attractive shelter for game which they could then kill: I can't imagine making a plan of such size. Rhododendrons were not made for the harsh Scottish climate. Botanists created a new variety, by combining North American and Spanish species brought back by the plantsmen. Now it is prolific, often blocking the path of other endemic flora. Poor trees, poor mosses, poor ferns. Still it is very romantic, this nowhere plant. Colour swaggering through everything. No, I won't be blamed for my affinity with monsters. I am not the one destroying trees.

Rhododendrons are a highly invasive species. Why do you call it romantic? Pink and red and purple are the colours of romance. You can see the effect that romance has on the body. Small bruises appear on the skin. Tender to the touch. Marbled flesh. I dreamt I fell in love with a flower which grew from under your fingernails. We used heavy machinery with a long hydraulic arm to extract the flower from the root. A number of days later small bruises appeared on your fingers and the backs of your hands. It was very romantic.

In the other place, the place of strange-time, I am sneez-
ing, I am underwater, I am watched. By things that don't
belong in the sea: cameras, people, a mop leaning against a
wall. Unusual eyes. This must mean that the other place is an
aquarium. Nose pressed against the ridge of a tortoise shell,
the gills of a shark . I like the hard logic of glass in between
everything. When I spell aquarium I always add a 'c', as if I 'm
holding onto a cough. I recognise that strong aquarium smell:
water trying too hard, forced through tacky f ilters. Water is
given too much responsibility. (No, the water is not my body
!) My mother tells me often of the time I broke a large, rare
shell at the aquarium out near Loch Lomond. She watched
as I lifted it from a shallow tank that imitated a rock pool,
small waves breaking against the glass. I pulled it close to
my chest, touching my forehead to its pinkness. Then lifted
it up, elbows straight in the air, and smashed it against the
tiled floor. Afterwards I asked her for punishment. She does
not remember that in the chaos I slipped a fragment of shell
inside my sock .
(I had been forced to wear a dress and
it did not have any pockets.)

Tim Knights
Matthew Kinlin
Christopher Owen

Pavilion

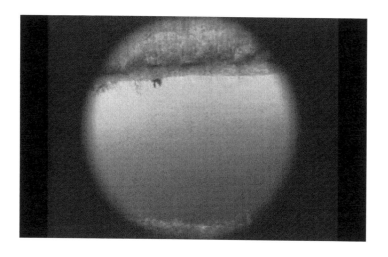

Early to rise, woken by the most cracked iPhone,
Cold water shave but it's all right.
'Put a shirt on you'll have queers lookin' at yer', Hmm I think
you might have said that earlier.
I might go and join them you know
As I'm lonely and I think that
they Like it as much as I do.

A simple life freely chosen is a source of strength.

POLICE REPORT

Missing Persons Case: Rudi Simmonds
Evidence: handwritten journal entry
Notes: article discovered in a local zoo

I met somebody who could be helpful. I was walking up the mound from the waterfall and found myself surrounded by ferns. They smelt the same as the ferns near my old house, the scent was so strong I panicked and nearly passed out. In my sun dazed delirium, an apparition of a portly man approached me, he was wearing hiking boots with thick rolled up socks. His biceps were chubby and substantial and had what looked like a llama tattooed amateurly on his forearm. I think he could see I was struggling in the heat so he sat with me. With his presence, the cast of light shining through the ferns grew stronger and the scent became overwhelming.

The next thing I knew we were rubbing shoulders in the pool at the top of the waterfall, looking over the edge, the rush of water bursting over the edge not quite strong enough to take us with it. Through the ripples of the water I could see that he was wearing yellow shorts that were too small for him, he let me graze my hand across his bulge, the closeness of his breath kept me at ease.

I remember looking directly at the sun then. I don't know if it was just the ripples in the water, but I looked back to what before resembled his canary yellow pants and now they were almost phosphorescent like an alien or a toxic jellyfish. Their yellow was mesmerising under the water, like they were dancing in the current. Almost to distract me from what I'd seen, he turned me around and pushed my face over the edge of the waterfall then forced his dick inside me. I was scared I'd lose my grip and imagined the current sending our bodies flying over the edge of the rock, hurtling towards the rock face 100 metres below, merging together on bloody impact.
Dead, but content.

He shot his load inside me, then pulled out, washing his willy in the water before pulling back up his shorts, which were back to their muted yellow hue. My fear was that he'd leave me back where he found me, haunted by the ferns, but we've been together a few nights now and I think we're going to stick together, I think we're both headed in the same direction.

Two strange things of note:

a)   He carries a small ceramic llama in his possession. When I look at it time disappears, the sky turns black and I completely zone out.

b)   Night by night there's a mist that encroaches closer and closer to where we're sleeping on the grass, it looks like it's come from a theatrical smoke machine. Tonight is the closest it's been.

He pulls his hands up into the air and backwards over his shoulders, like he's turning inside out. He does it on the grass, his shadow flickering across the pavilion wall beneath green and rusted beams, hung above the cool stone.

There are many clues in the pavilion:

1.   A pair of red Converse trainers. The laces are knotted together and unable to be separated despite concerted effort. Found hanging from the pavilion roof.

2.   An unopened bottle of Fanta Limon balanced on the green railings at the exact point the sun reaches 2:03pm. They sit and watch it eclipsed behind the bottle momentarily.

3.   A used copy of John Milton's Paradise Lost in the litter bin, shoved in amongst the large pizza boxes. Books V and VI have been torn out. No writing inside.

He takes off his shirt and falls asleep upon the grass, dreams about Doctor Manhattan entering the test chamber—blue, carousel clouds pouring from Manhattan's mouth. He wakes up and brushes twigs from his stomach, the hair across his shoulders.

They lie upon a brick wall and listen to murmuring traffic. There are buses streaming in the distance like silver arrows. The buses run to Parkhead, filled with men sat in emerald football shirts, pie-eyed and bulging into the future.
Spiders run into the cracks around the base of the concrete stairs, some filled with cobwebs that sway loosely in the wind. Others, they peer inside to find dead ants, a pink condom tied and filled with sperm.

A boy with a lip piercing tears up magazines, scatters their excellent smiles across the ground: Dua Lipa, Billie Eilish,

Armie Hammer rotting in a Wuxi hotel. In the centre of the pavilion, a mirror and a chair.

Bottles in a Tesco carrier bag: Blue VK, Tropical Fruits VK, Watermelon VK. They smoke weed until they feel sick. They burn a photograph at 4.09pm with a yellow Bic lighter.

Someone has taken down Paradise Lost from the stone shelf behind the mirror and is reading aloud from Book IV: O sun, to tell thee how I hate thy beams. They pull down their shorts to show off bright orange pubes.

He sits in the chair before the mirror at dusk. The others ask him to look into the glass and make three confessions about his grandmother.

1.   She believed a vampire lived in Govan—had seen a sarcophagus in a shop window.

2.   She died on her own birthday like an idiot.

3.   She kept a pot of lavender on the windowsill.

They watch an episode of the X-Files on an iPhone. Mulder's voice through the darkness.

Dear diary, today my heart leapt when Agent Scully suggested spontaneous human combustion.

Thanks for getting in touch, I'm glad you enjoyed my pictures. Just to check, how old are you? It's great to be in touch with someone from the United Kingdom, did you know we share a queen? We love Coronation Street out here too, we watch it in our conservatory every Thursday afternoon.

Are you gay or curious? If you know that you're gay I would recommend joining a local group, is there a Christian missionary group for gay teenagers in your locale? When I was your age joining one made all the difference. I met like-minded people, we travelled to impoverished communities together and it really changed my life. I felt I belonged and could go out into the world without feeling scared of who I was. I think it's a great idea for someone of your age.

How is the weather over there? I've been walking the maple trail this morning, but New Brunswick is still grey.

Stay in touch,
Bignick (Nicholas)

With a timid friend in tow, he's broken into father's ceramics workshop and stolen his ironstone asteroid pots. His father had arranged them to resemble a city skyline, they were the only pieces the boy liked because they were shiny. Watched eagerly by spectators from the pavilion, he arrives in the field next door and places them on the designated spot in the centre. He takes the set of explosives purchased at the army surplus store and places them decoratively in and around the pieces.

Without thinking too hard, he signals to the pavilion, lights the fuse and takes his friend's hand.

A series of metallic, sharp explosions cut through the air as thousands of vitreous shards of tenmoku red, cobalt lustre and alkaline egyptian blue cut through the sultry atmosphere, the local blackbirds fly panicked towards the sun and collectively, the spectators pupils dilate with excitable fear as the shimmering fragments rain down on the land, scattering evenly throughout the field.

Now in the moonlight, the field glows!

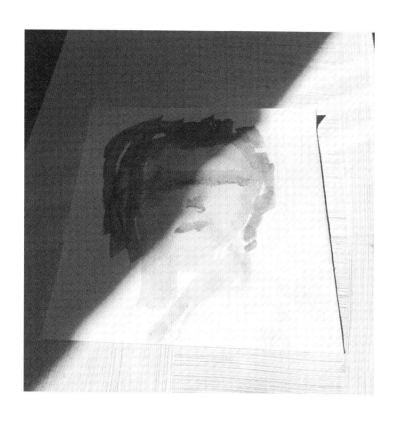

sunburn beginning to glow
a horoscope tattooed on the back of his calf
mother said his birthstone was yellow topaz

cabin at the end of a pier
faded photographs of coronation street phantoms
violet carson, pat phoenix

video favourited on xtube
david in an aberdeen travelodge
the blue repeating carpet

when the chair faces the mirror
he can see much further
into september (sapphires)

song about buchanan bus station
wee roddy fae rockhampton avenue
teleports into lake texcoco

dragon lines underneath
liver line along the middle of his palm
mercury below the little pinkie

he made him take his clothes off
and stand in the long grass
so embarrassed he wanted to cry

a rizla of amphetamine sherbert
lungs accelerated into daffodils
he laughs and urinates a stream of light

one kiss is all it takes
fallin' in love with me, possibilities
i look like all you need

Just before the fall of man we bought some land,
And shared it with some fellas to grow something to eat,
We put our backs into making the fields yield crops and the
barn our home,
Mucked out the llamas for a whole fucking day,
The evenings spent studying the stars,
A good stock of lube, and in the yard a sling,
We were happy labouring forever in the great taskmaster's
eye.

Lucy Cash
Luke Pell

to the southside and back again (things I didn't photograph)

long black socks with rainbow trim queuing outside the Co-op
  Bite Me sandwich bar facing Serene Coffee House
garden hose washing taxi in hands of irked man in orange-check shirt
    d o g s e g g s graffiti on concrete pillar across Bells' bridge
wrestle of man & child with Wendy house balanced on wheelbarrow
      radio & striped deckchair on mown lawn &
    birdsong with blackbird in dead of day,
      Love & Squalor no longer
    greyhound on lead, yawning
      lilac & blue boards covering glass front of closed Valhalla's Goat
highland terrier in rusty mesh basket on front of yellow Raleigh
    horse chestnut tree
  chestnut horse
    gold crash helmet tricycling up hill, behind knees jogging backwards
an amber, sleeping squirrel

(I didn't because
they weren't
mine to take;
they belong
elsewhere & to
the city & to
the light
in all its
verticality;
or maybe
I mean
in all its
time, or all
its particles;
or they belong
to themselves,
undisturbed.)

reached &

attempt

but
felt
for

to
be

undreamt

(some nights)

333

a factory for carpets, flats

run away to be in love with battered
mars bars & no end of night

a brick, a thud, a shower of glass

sparks

that you thought that he'd got out of
all of this

a motor mechanics built
for: unwritten books

so many dances; so many un-gloved

Maryhill, following the Forth and Clyde

I'm trying to trick myself
temple gasworks' remains

        he swelled up   like
                                     a wolf

into remembering how
thirteen nests scaffolding a birch tree

                       not just

I used to do it
marsh marigolds yellow at the water's edge

                       his fur

Now everyone else is doing it
river up full, lone swan gliding

& with such ease
bright green moth caterpillar, hanging

                     but his

Not easy to feel what you can't see —
by a thread

I forgot to remove
branch of catkins

the shoes of my
leaf fall, soil

voice, to meet you
a line of ants

with a tender attending

body

whole

Coming out from Cambuslang crossing to Govan, fair
and

Cloud.

A crowd   Sun

Blue-faced, dial glint in gold

Coal and butter   Held — in hand — pink

The rush

        about feet
        about mouths

A line, a clump, a throng, a procession up & in a gate
an arch, a bridge of breaths let go across

There was a ram

there

once

at the bend

&

bags

& sweat

& metal

337

We stood looking out, someone said
— you, I think —
if you aren't afraid
step closer
to the front

                        pipe
                        & steam

                        & pole
                        & towels

The edge, a precipice, small verge of
green, spilling over old stone

Walk

                        thrown

I did.

               in

at the city of the dead

a north east wind
for a seagull to turn in

energy doesn't die

ivy pale with fatigue after
a long night with bluebells

it transforms

magpie sentinel sheltering
in the long grass

    locked; tolled; taught;   alert;

horizon lowers its sights,
winds ambush

the shadow of an elm tree
with heart

shakes;

alert;

obliteration

sighs & quivers & dissolving

& you & me seeking solace
with the ones who no longer
have to hear words of --

my eyes rest
in folds and folds and folds,
cloth decorating urns &
      angel wings

energy doesn't die, it alters

On getting up one morning & finding my way, out of your flat

in the night, Raeberry Street

blind   or, the light

    cat lying in dip of quilt between two bodies

    sleepiness of air between one room & another

               in the buttonholes of the covers & green

                    a branch or a bird   house

    yellow rug, still bright even under the night

               I'm unsure, it was early for me &

    dark green leaves waiting patiently for day

my fingers

the cat called
the belle rang &
the shower sprayed up
the un-tiled wall &
into the litter tray

    glow of three milk-white chairs guarding kitchen table

tired roof of building hugging its windows close

I saw dust   or breath or bits of what were

tiny chess pieces of spires & minarets beyond
           your or mine, or his

gleam of glass water container
    skin

chalk-white beaker next to docile sink
             floating/

hands a familiar hold for shape of ceramic & water
           falling/

between the gorse of the ground spun &
the spire & the slats stacked beyond   flailing/
a small pane, before
I turned
        floating

dreaming, slowly filling beaker
water dreaming, shaking; tiny pond quivering as the moon tries to pull it
closer –
              the cup
              the locks
              with your keys.

first time at The Arches

— Anna; before you & STILL — my first Glasgow gig,
a bloom of bodies, words; tangles of skin & muscle all
new new new freckles on the flesh of my thoughts;
pretend kissing to Nico singing deutschland uber alles,
the stones in her voice tethering me to the ground
which otherwise I would float free from with
shame & fear & excitement because it felt real and
this was exhibit in the dark of the day, an artificial
night with no end, with no end but a
border to elsewhere & an othering &
eat the seeds with your eyes &
have your ears pour sound &
this city feels the shape of me
& I —

&

&

&

Last time, at The Arches

pipe works and private party smoking in
the yellow white, bent back, bent over
bent between bricks & split, liquor in a
puddle that spilled inside my sock & toes &
package, bags I carried east to west on the bus beneath
my seat with my pants, on my back, in the lift, in the
locker in the corner, in the room, that
was locked, on the rail with a rubber
strapped key & a bell to Ade & tell Janice
it was time between shifts, after work, after
hours, after trips, for business that
became, more constant, before & after
Nigel —still — sessions that started that summer
in the spring the rain trickled

Tessa Berring
Kathrine Sowerby

Are You With Me?

Romance means a mysterious excitement of love
It can also mean a mysterious remoteness from life

The setting - a fairground, lights, and
unconvincing beer tents
Stalls of sweet and savoury

Shall we buy a macaroon?

How the simplest recipes draw attention to
themselves
How easy we are!

I remember the mixing bowl, the warm paper bag
The man selling them, not him exactly

What a good idea to focus on one product

Sentimental means tender or sad or nostalgic
or all three

Days before there was a man sniffing an aerosol in the same
    spot

I love the smell of dog, and the smell of oil and hairspray

I love how people fill a space
Only to empty it later

Perfume counters, sleeping bags, rivers, cemeteries

It's impossible to remember
Which exit to take

Whether to go with or against the crowd

I depended on your coming too
or on your being already there

It was the basement wasn't it?
No, maybe the bookshop

How terrible memory is
if it isn't sugary enough

Romantic enough?

Bookshop/basement
I know we enjoyed it

The streets look the same too

Some lead into the woods (if you walk far
enough)
Some lead straight into the canal

That's too tragic! Try again

Anywhere but here! Or the opposite -
A comfortable chair (Is that cowardly?)
I'm talking about belonging

It gets to fever pitch in some circles
(My heart belongs to ....)

It can be very romantic

What is your favourite belonging?
There's a question

It used to be a tiny Russian pot

The man on the train said I was 'the dreamy one'

You know what I'd like to do?

I'd like to walk barefoot on those coconut hills

Have you seen the footage of lava pouring into the sea?

You have to be in a boat to see it
Or at home in bed, walking about

All the lights, all the people looking for something

I like tight knit spaces and breaking out of them.
Like the plants I saw today, breaking through
cracks in the wall

Break hearts!

And a picture of a young man with a scar the
length of his torso

And there's Tessa!

The station was busy and half finished
The gold ceiling, part installed

I always think I'll fall in love during rush hour -

And there won't be time to enjoy it

The plummet

I am usually at home rushing to make tea. Dinner?
I call it tea. Is that what you meant?

Tea at 6 every night, which is why I miss so much

Potatoes and melted butter

But that night, let's call it night
there were macaroons

Luxury means a state of great comfort and
elegance often involving expense

A city should be elegant
A city is full of anger

I like the Georgia O'Keefe quote about being scared all her
    life
but how she never let it stop her from doing what she wanted

Perhaps she would have wanted different things
if she hadn't been scared?

Sometimes people are stopped
whether they are scared or not

To be equal as possible (and notice the difference)
To be human (we don't have a choice!)

That's my least favourite phrase -
Be human!

Please fill out this form – where did you come from?

Being in a city you don't know is an adventure

I come to the city then leave
I was here. I was there

I am on the verge of leaving all the time
And it's not easy being the one who stays

Kathrine

My train is here, do you mind if I go

I remember that...everyone comes and goes
in a stagger

I got bored and bought chips

Then I saw another friend and was polite for a
while

She told a lie

Accidental meetings when you want to be
anonymous

Pigeons

They come in the morning and peck the coconut

Which way is the river?
The canal?

That way – past the houses with the clarinets

Then the windows and the rose beds
The cafe with the young stars and the old records

Heartbeats are loud

I have no idea where we are

Wouldn't it be nice to walk vertically

I was reading about clouds you see – days of no
clouds being good days
Days of no doors being bad days

I can't see the coconut any more
My memory is thin like a cobweb

People like to make sense

I wonder why?

Future means something that doesn't exist -
impossible days

We could get high on that, and ridiculous

Let's get drunk in a crowd
Let's be angry

There are trains that go by with no passengers
A big red sculpture on a mirrored plinth

The reflection makes a heart
and all the windows are open

Press the air, said the poet
and I don't know what she meant

Nothing matters. Only air

Not the walls, not the words, not the romance, not
the hospital

Permission to breathe?

I'm lost now
Even though I know this place well

Cut yourself off from knowing
(That sounds like self-help manuals!)

Helpful phrases like

'Are you with me?'

Anjeli Caderamanpulle
Joanne Lee

Dear Joanne

I am on Amelia's rooftop and a bit drunk. I ate tempura seaweed (salted egg flavour) and had a few gin and soda cans. I love the way snacks are packaged here. The packets are so big; the metallic plastic is sturdy and the air within them is so tight. I feel like a youtuber buying these random snacks at 7/eleven like I have content to produce (TRYING ASIAN SNACKS?? :P :K) I have purchased at least three things each night knowing I will eat one and leave the others for later, or maybe keep as a gift for someone. Do people enjoy getting snacks for a souvenir?

Every meal I have had here has been incredible. Amelia also loves to eat and try different food and it's lovely to share this experience with her. I am not usually a big food sharer, but I love the culture of ordering everything and trying it. My love for salt is being satiated and then some, but I still have the need to go and buy snacks after every single meal.

I woke up quite late today as I think the 8-hour time difference hit me. I feel more purpose when I'm away. I always have the fear of missing out on something incredible and not doing the best thing when I'm on holiday somewhere I know I might not visit again.
I woke up at 10:00, walked aimlessly around the city and almost passed out at 17:30 waiting for Amelia at a fountain in

a giant shopping centre.

I had spent last night on the terrace drinking Asahi and thinking about living here. I hate that this is the time I decide to do it when coronavirus is real and ultimately changing the city (hopefully temporarily). It would be worth knowing more from locals how the virus and the weird media involvement is affecting them. People here seem super practical about it, but maybe there is more hysteria to what I can see? I saw that the UK is at 50 cases and Hong Kong has just reached 100... it seems to be spreading a lot faster there.

I tried to go to the White Cube, but it was by appointment only. I can't really understand why all of the art here has shut down when it seems like not much else has? When I was walking around yesterday, I stumbled upon Tai Kwun when I went up the mid-level escalators. Colonial buildings are so sinister. Tai Kwun is a nice place to look at, especially when they have been renovated, but also exist as a gentrified place for corporate office workers to go for happy hour. I don't really know what to think about it as I don't know the angle that it's coming from (mama lets research.) You can tell loads of money has been put into it, the historical stuff was kind of vague but also within the timeline of world history, so a bit overwhelming lol. Strange curation alert. All of the exhibition spaces at Tai Kwun had been closed, and when I walked through Hong Kong Park, the visual arts centre there was also shut. The Gagosian seems to be closed indefinitely?

It was 16:00 and after I was squashed by the fancy White Cube Foyer, I spent most of my day on the pavement scrolling through restaurant reviews. Google reviews here are so funny... they'll list everything bad with the place but ultimately say the food was delicious and give five stars.

I went to a traditional bakery and had a bun with some meat and cheese and some pastries. I will probably go back tomorrow. I went to a restaurant and sat down but realised I had been given a westerner's menu and everything looked quite bad... (spag bol...etc.) So naturally, being an international food blogger, I went to McDonalds. I heard Hong Kong has the best McDonalds? It was ok to be honest... I really wanted to love her. There were some interesting options (pork cutlet? Standard burger but with an egg?), but I panicked and got fried chicken.

It was a bit of a nothing day, but sometimes eating and walking can be so good for you.

Anjeli

Dear Anjeli,

I have copied and pasted ur email onto a word doc so that my screen is filled with ur words and will eventually fill with mine too. Getting snacks and doing a shop when im away is one of my favourite things to do ever. I am excited to receive some of ur fave snacks as a souvenir – which I think make a very good gift. I am so happy that you're enjoying the food and like the sharing experience of it esp with being seated with strangers – which feels very Hong Kong and cosmopolitan. Communal eating without having to talk to anyone, you're never truly alone in that city.

I know what you mean about loving salt, they have very good crunchy salty things over there. Have you tried shrimp chips yet? They're like a puffed corn crisp in the shape of a prawn. With a savoury snack I feel like I could eat them forever without feeling sick. Maybe it's the crunch or the savouriness that allows my brain to register it as proper food?

Does this my writing sound like me? I love that you are just wandering around the city. Hong Kong doesn't really feel like a city where you can just slowly stroll cause it has such an ever present manic energy. But maybe that's what makes it feel extra like you're on holiday while everyone else is always rushing around u – like in a slow mo 00's music video. Also I think you should watch *In the Mood for Love* while you're there, it's my fave film I think and its set in 50s HK. It has a real restless longing and a hazy heat to it that I think you'll like.

I think you would really suit living in HK and tbh rather you than some awful finance bro. Eventually I want to live there too! But I think that I will be in Glasgow for a little while longer. Coronavirus truly is real, my dad just got back and is self-isolating for 2 weeks – which makes it sound more serious that it needs to be. Do you think you will too when you get back?

Its no great loss that you didn't get to go see those galleries esp the White Cube. I think the reason major art galleries and the frieze have been shut down / cancelled is because they're all like white western galleries who aren't really a real part of HK life.

I am glad that you are doing but lots of eating and walking, you're like a modern "flaneur" lol. I love being in Hong Kong sm but it's a place where you can def feel the remains of colonialism. I guess it's not so much remains but in the current landscape. I guess as my family don't stay in the central bit and I've never experienced Hong Kong as a tourist. I've not seen as many colonial buildings. The timelines of the place do feel quite overwhelming. It feels like a dreamscape when I try to imagine the place in my head. So dense and vast and liveable as a city but with such extremes in place. I think it is one of the most expensive cities in the world where the cost of living is truly wild.

I think that's the rule, if the food is excellent nothing else matters, cause you're in and out so quickly. Not a place for slow lingering eaters! Have you tried the egg tarts or the bubble waffles yet? I also love a holiday McDonalds – they have fun fruity drinks that are always class.

This is quite waffly and I think I am relying on your writing/ editing experience to tease out the bits that are sparky and relevant. Next time I am writing back immediately and remember to send me food pics.

Until soon and with much love,
Joanne xxx

Dear Joanne,

I am sorry I haven't replied sooner to your email. Don't worry about 18 hours as I took a whole week omg. I kept wanting to take my laptop out with me but I went to the beach and thought that might be stupid. The jet lag got to me after that, and there's been a few humidity sleeps. I think I jinxed myself by asking to write every day.

It did sound like you, it's super interesting to see how other people write. It's weird to have to structure your thoughts when it's usually so conversational through texting. How did you find writing this? I don't know a lot about your art so I would love to see some of your work if you're able to send it over. I used to write long emails to friends when I was younger, I read some of them the other day and they were so funny.

Ugh the salt here is so good. My chin and cheeks are puffed up like those shrimp puffs. I also puffed up tenfold when I was basically having anaphylaxis. I think what was scary about it was the embarrassment, I didn't want to stress anyone out even though I was basically dying. The lady who sold us the spring roll wanted us to buy them all. As soon as I ate it and knew something was wrong... but I still swallowed it... I can't believe how dumb I can be to be agreeable.

Hong Kong felt like a place that I could stroll for hours just looking at things. I guess that's the effect of the protests and Coronavirus, people are inside so it gave me space within the city. When I came back from hospital, Amelia's flatmate and her girlfriend were out on the terrace with their friends. It was interesting meeting people who were not from the corporate world who were still able to live in Hong Kong (maybe because of rich parents or English teaching jobs.) One of their friends was American (and despite what I am going to write...was very nice lol) and had written a lot about the protests and spoken to protesters when they were at their peak. Amelia's flatmate said to him "it's so valuable to have your perspective...", and I was sitting there breathless and dizzy from adrenaline and anti-histamines but totally confused by that comment.

There is some value in having someone from the outside report on situations far away – to be honest, I didn't really understand the impact and amount of time that the protests had being going on for. People only vaguely knew about it from conversations I had in the UK and it seems that even a lot of ex-pats don't understand Hong Kong as a fully formed place. It's a bit gross. Amelia's boss told us she has lived in Hong Kong for 11 years and doesn't know any Cantonese. Their reporter friend didn't feel like a voyeur in that respect, mining for content, and his stories presented the protesters as people, but I was sitting there thinking... ok big woop.

You're right about the White Cube and other galleries. I think that's what I am trying to get at, there's so many spots that are so Chinese and then all of a sudden, a white gap of western culture that doesn't necessarily feel wrong, but strange. It sounds like what you're describing, this looping back to something unrecognisable. Amelia was telling me about Macao and I am upset I can't visit. Hong Kong seems to have this concept of third culture at it's heart. Please tell me if I am wrong lol – but all of the young Chinese people I met there had an international backstory.

I am back in the UK now, thinking about coronavirus, and how I was able to walk through Heathrow airport with literally no questions asked. My brother has the flu and is infecting everything in sight. I have been awake since 4am - and I am trying to stay awake but it's hard and I really don't want to. I also want to watch Chinese films! I haven't seen any Wong Kar Wai films. I felt the longing hard in Hong Kong. So many couples, and such a beautiful place to fall in love if you're a young professional LOL. I wasn't longing for anything in particular while I was away. I think maybe I needed a break from my tragic love life in Glasgow. I loved Hong Kong so much, and there's so much I need to tell you still :]

Dearest Anjeli,

I'm so glad to have you back safe and sound in Glasgow, although the past two days coronavirus PANIC has fully set in for me. How are you finding being back? Again sorry for replying so late to you - waiting on my fish fingers to cook as I'm writing to you. It's so funny I used to email my friends all the time too when I was little - think maybe that texts used to be too expensive or something? Maybe that's how we should format our emails to each other too? Fun fonts and colours and emojis etc. Truly a special way of communicating.

It does feel super weird to be writing so casually but within this email structure cause I know that eventually this will lead to something bigger and more formal (?) I think that we should do an art swap and come back together to discuss. I have realised that I fucking hate talking about my work because it feels so mired up in shame and discomfort. Lol because it feels so personal, and it came directly from me. It is something that I am def not very good at.

I miss that good msg too - now when I think of salt / msg it also makes me think of Euan's aromat seasoning stuff. Maybe we should also start incorporating it into our seasoning. I can't imagine anything scarier than almost dying in a country far away. Hahaha I can relate to that so much almost dying from embarrassment rather than kick up a fuss. What were you thinking about in the hospital? You look incredible and glowing in the photo you sent me of u in hospital!

I am so glad that you had the time and space to be able to just walk around Hong Kong like that - it's such a rare thing to be able to navigate the city space like that. Maybe this is a new type of tourism/ travel experience - disaster holiday - feels like we're witnessing the change over into the future. Everything we know now is changing so quickly. Sorry for how late this reply is again but doing anything but panicking seems futile. It sounds like you were hanging out with some v interesting people out in HK but also like yikes. I think you're right tho I don't have insightful thing to say apart from white ppl being the worst. It's a strange mindset to be in - not quite knowing what is colonial / colonised / ours / theirs.

I hope that you've not done too much yearning in the time of coronavirus. But this has just made everything feel more precarious and sadder and scary. Sending you all the love and company while you're finishing up your coronavirus self-isolation.

Until soon and with much love and care,
Joanne

Joanne,

Ok so it's now August, and nothing and everything has happened in between. I like to think that this experience and situation has brought us closer together. I loved talking on Facetime almost every morning. Quarantine seems to be a period of heavy upheaval for so many, trying to get at *something* - using time more effectively or allowing yourself to have a break.

Anyway, I wrote this a few days before I came back to London? I didn't write the date so I am not too sure but it was after Euan's birthday:

I'm so sorry I stopped replying. I have found it so hard to get back into what I need to do until the last moment. I know you can relate. Why is it that the most microscopic of errands feels astronomically difficult? Similarly, the smallest of things has the largest impact. I've been obsessive about circular movements and repeating patterns - which makes sense, I guess.

I don't know what it is that gave me an allergic reaction on Wednesday - so in the interest of not wasting food - I have decided to have a small amount of the lamb biryani I ordered to see if I will be sick. Living life on the edge as per usual *(this sentence is cringe but I was having a near death experience.)*

Weirdly, I forget about my allergic reaction in Hong Kong and felt more doomed due to COVID being a reality in Hong Kong at the time.

I was telling Iona recently that perhaps what I feel most upset about is how abstract situations can feel when I am not directly involved. I can detach when things get hard. I want to be present and overthink being present. I feel disgustingly guilty about that and then I feel guilty for being so self-involved. Being in a hospital in Hong Kong and thinking I might die away from my family and everyone. I think feeling so anxious means being self-involved.

Sometimes I want to just tell people I have checked out completely - that I am trying to iron out everything and spread it out to try and mend myself, and as such am on hiatus until I get there. It's becoming more evident to me that healing is ongoing and I need to get out of my head like Ru Paul says (my free therapist) so I can be present for others.

At the hospital they told me I had to pay £100 to see a doctor and then I had to think if that was worth it. Again, I was dying lol. I decided that was ok after I realised it was only getting worse. I think what I am trying to come to terms with is this lack of balance (or aggressively acting in extremes.) It's not sustainable and so draining. Some days I wake up and I feel "cured", happy and ready to give other people advice on how they should be living because I have worked it out. The next day I will wake up and be aware that I exist in my body and that it's slowly decaying while I live within it. I am sorry for being so emo and weird, but I am trying to get at something. Being in London is really hard.

I think it's in coming to terms with not everything can be 100% amazing all the time and trying to get on with it. Being caught in the same arguments and stories and jokes. Sometimes it's nice and comforting, but most of the time it makes me feel like a maniac. Recently I just want to jump out of my skin with how uncomfortable I feel. How stupid people are around me. This is old news but Twitter and other periphery stuff makes me feel so quick to react. Is it bad or good - does it even matter lol. Everything feels so meaningless, it seems that anything we make is geared towards a reaction and then we discard it and we don't try to understand why or what it is.

Tick, tick, tick, X on a conveyor belt. Let me know if this is getting too Fight Club. I have watched too many machisimo deep bro films recently and I am trying to understand music I have missed before. I can actually bore myself with how I feel about art. I thought about tweeting the other day, 'do i know lots about film and music because I like it, or because I want to dunk on boys.' I think you're really good at working out these kinds of contrasting feelings. I like that you just cut through the bullshit where I can idolise famous people for no reason beyond a gut feeling.

Anyway, I did get sick again from the biriyani and got scared about the way allergic reactions can start up again even if it's out of your body. I called 111 and had to explain the situation. The lady on the phone was incredulous *"so you had an allergic reaction to this a day ago and you decided to have more of it, and now you feel sick again?"*

I used it as an excuse to take a sick day from work. It felt good because I was technically telling the truth.

Here's a poem I wrote since we last spoke:

        I only feel like writing on the tube
arterial, where my blood warms
flows to extremity
feel it circle back
I feel someone next to me
tightness leaving
relax into sour blankness
watching the map
no exhalation in completion
tension is in the imagined
grey and tired
the person opposite is probably someone

since leaving london i have imagined
that beyond it is
wide open fields and spaces

toes in grass and the banks
fresh water cleaner than the tap
more nourishing than anyone living

cauterize box room appendages
razor thin bathrooms and cracked open windows
no time with people i love
spending it all with what i hate
feeling shame in the bottom of the bus
kissing in my parent's garden
sweating,
I don't know how else to say
I am trying to get at something

Anjeli

Hello Anjeli,

Omg its now the 1st of September and the evening. But I'm so happy that our months long email chain is finally coming to fruition. I find myself writing my replies very urgently and hungry physically and mentally cause I'm so used to just being still and forgetting to feed myself and my brain.

I love that we talked everyday at the start of lockdown too - I feel like it helped keep me sane and grounded, that I wasn't the only one manically in my flat just thinking and being chaotic. It just hit me that its now been like half a year of lockdown. I also have a difficult time grasping and under-standing time and how I move through it. I stay the same and time happens around me.

You are such a gifted and funny story teller - I feel like I was there beside you holding in my laughter as the NHS 24 women asked you - *"so you had an allergic reaction to this a day ago and you decided to have more of it, and now you feel sick again?"*. I scream!!!

I get what you mean because I am also extremely neurotic - but I never use that term lol it feels v Woody Allen, New York film speak where everyone sees a shrink but is still a massive dickhead. When I was younger I use to imagine wee scenarios in my head - like what would I do if I was suddenly in a car crash? How would I react if all my family suddenly died? I use to think that was v sick and morbid and it was my secret guilty pleasure. But I think that maybe it was just my tiny baby brain way of giving me control and a strange coping mechanism. Sometimes I still catch myself doing it. I think this is how I learned to be a person - by watching soaps and movies. I feel like I'm only really starting to figure out who I really am without adding or embellishing my personality with media tropes. I was a pretty insufferable teen I think because of this. SO antsy.

That's so funny I also have a holiday medical emergency. Idk if I ever told you about this. But years ago, when I fancied M like mad I went to France in the summer to see them and it was so dreamy and felt like I was really living in the most cinematic sense. Being around sexy French ppl all day and eating breakfast on their pals balcony in the blazing sunshine. We were beside the sea and no one told me that there's so many mosquitos and I was bitten so much that one of the bites got infected. One of the bites started to blister and swell on my knee, so finally we went to the doctors and I got prescribed antibiotics... all in all I had to splash £140 on the doctor and the antibiotics all b/c I didn't have my EHIC insurance card. Truly sad to think that maybe my romantic life peaked with that trip to France.

Lately my head is so *******fried******** like that huge kfc we had last night. I'm slowly moving out my depression phase I feel but I honestly don't know how people find the time and energy to do literally anything at all. The only reason that I no longer let myself spend all day in bed is because I know that it only makes me shiter and sadder. She is displaying self growth! I thought that the camping trip away would have provided me with at least 2/3 days worth of feeling happy and content but honestly, it's just been straight back to feeling shite. But in a much more manageable way I feel. Like I'm playing the easy mode of a video game. But being so present and comfortably in my body and properly being in nature and letting the natural order of things carry me over the weekend has made me realise that my day to day lifestyle doesn't work for me at all... Just need to figure out how to live beside the sea and in the city. It was just so nice waking up early and when it got cold and dark, we could build a fire and then eat. There was a rhythm that had to be followed, a presence and awareness that I was really taking care of all my needs.

No time with people i love
Spending all of it with things i hate
Feeling shame in the bottom of the bus
Kissing in my parents garden
Sweating my upper lip furry no one will see it
And i want i dont know how else to say
I am trying to get at something

I'll leave u with the last stanza of ur tube poem which I liked very much and sums up how I'm feeling.
with much love and until soon,
Joanne xxxxx

Kirsty Dunlop
Maria Sledmere

a little kilo of dreams
27/3/20

Of course, I was trying to land a plane inside another plane...
backwards. I told you (you were a blank yet familiar face),
that I had no experience of flying planes. But this is no
real plane, you explained to me, this is a toy plane and
we are only dust swirling in the air. With a soft delayed
breath, you vanished before me without even saying
goodbye. I wanted to look at the landscape outside, find
some sense of comfort in recognising Glasgow: sandstone
buildings, the Clyde, Kelvingrove, but I was still inside
another plane, dark, metallic and claustrophobic. I just
knew there was going to be an explosion but this seemed
to be no longer something to fear; I only had to let my
body blend into the air and accept that no one could see
me, not even you.

Airstrip

Bruised by
the travel of air
Typing, typing
What doesn't land
or translate
on the same street
I stayed awake listening
to my body
blend
with birdsong
There is a Glasgow
delayed like breath
there is nothing
but dust
Here
I am imminent
in the only air of my Blank
Not taking off
my slip
so dark
I had worn the night
to sluttishness, claustro
as a body
in transit
with several invisibles
my soft breath

delayed
onscreen, the Clyde
was a scrollbar
to slide down
bicycle honeyed
You remember
the infinity plane
at the end of *Remainder*
I want to say
bye bye, bye bye!
The sky is the colour
inside the sky

3/4/20

Dreamt about sleeping /,.;klpAQ~Z|"?
?> IN BUT IT was just paranoia. I was talking to M. about this strange phenomenon and she was like but do you know they've shut down the English department. And I was like Yeah but I'm in Creative Writing, right? But they were subsumed of course. I freaked out a little bit then I saw a moment of '68 liberation where we could form our own department and share the good junkpiles of our intellect. I also dreamt I was lying in the front garden of Daisybank unable to move in a state of paralysed bliss, and there were all these alarm clock voiceovers from Next Bikes. They would announce every new £2.50 service, and the free NHS service where you just swiped your NHS card to use it for free. I adore the smell of coffee...What is it about a level of ENERGY this week. Have I been eating more sugar than usual? Some of the bikes had NHS-coloured tassels on them. It was like I could astral project from my paralysed lawn where I would move as a drone over everything. On the webcam I wanted to have something of value to talk about, *an event that had happened*. I could tell of my ransacked house, the mining of history, the emptying out of beautiful glassware which had once been negative space. So I will fail to scan and in doing so beautifully retain a degree of coarseness to the original drawing. It was good to just dream about imminent bike rides. The voiceover said YES, two of you might be spooning which will take even longer to move but...for me the cycle really adds sex appeal, I mean cycling, wow, I mean it really

adds to the human lure, I guess it's the speed and elegance...I want that lawn! toss bike away! I want to lie in a meadow. There's this bit about meadows in one of f.'s poems. One time Rob Macfarlane retweeted me on meadows, or did I dream that too? might rename my diary just THE COMMON or something, or should it be commons, aye, plural— yes a reference to Moten but also importantly just this idea of the common book, wildflowers. What do you think?...O I also know I was with D. in an abandoned hotel which was somehow Oran Mor related! ... ah and I've just unlocked another part of the dream, Okay so there was this weekly kind of lecture hall where I'd go to watch micro-theatre performances. they were kind of avant-garde in a good way. You got tokens for attending which would go towards your progress or something... there was this function on Instagram where you could sort of access a grid of everyone's faces to see their stories, but these were like livestreams so different from normal stories, Zoomlike, and we clicked on L.'s — she was singing alone really loudly and blithely, bless her — and D. used my phone to send a shiny eye react and I couldn't even explain that was him because I couldn't reveal we'd been out of quarantine together...

?>

aye, BUT
what do you think?
Can a shiny eye react explain
negative space
paralysed bliss
turning up the level of energy
Instagram
craving sugar more than usual
the liberated lawn
and the voiceover allure of another human
normal stories clicking
NHS state
paranoia of the frame
THE COMMON
wow,
all that creative writing
the value of talking
an event that just happened
this plural pretentious
how i fucking miss
the yes?
,.;klpAQ   ~Z|"?

look,
i want a grid of future selves,
the emptying out of all that reveal.

8/4/20

I dreamt we were back at Nice n Sleazy's, and I was just about to order twenty white russians. I didn't really want them but somehow it felt necessary. I searched for the friends to give the drinks to but the tables were empty. The only sound of life was one distant voice singing a Suzanne Vega song from the basement. I knew it was one of my favourite songs: 'Marlene on the Wall'. I tasted the milky texture on my tongue and I wanted to hold it there and not swallow. I shouldn't even be here, I was panicking. I must get to work. So I jumped in a taxi and glided gracefully along the motorways. The library was empty except for a woman who asked me to recommend some erotic fiction. I was happy to oblige. When I picked up the book (it was a classic title: Surgeon Takes Another Virgin), it began to swallow me whole. I was sticking to text, I was falling and I waited for the body to hit ground. I thought to myself: I am still waiting, I am still waiting and I am still falling through all this fiction.

Nice 'n' Eurydice

Sleaziest variable.
Orpheus with ice
in his arteries, to know
precisely this. That you would
hold Marlene to the standards of roses,
that you would motor
the way. That you would even
queue for it. I took paid
opportunities to die in the library.
That you would tattoo
such words from Vegas or Hades.
I was happy to oblige
with the handsome fist
to fall as though waiting
to fall. When you ask
I say "very much
in love." I wanted
the twenty white russians
of a Lorca sonnet,
a nineties classic;
the bad erotica
of looking back.

Ended up staying over at Amanda Seyfried's house in Kelvin-
side... I'm not sure how it happened, but I slept in her bed. The
flat was gorgeous and she had a small child who I witnessed her
talking to outside, she was saying to eat healthier and button-
ing the kid's puffy coat. Her flat doubled as Artisan Roast and
I put through an order which nobody made so after a while I
made it myself, this casual latte. I made too much and it was
watery and I kept spilling the unwanted milk all over the carpet
and having to mop it up. Amanda felt that she had to explain
to me why she was here in Glasgow of all places working as a
barista and she kept saying she wanted to give her child the
closest, most authentic start in life. I was at some funeral and
I saw ??? and she was huge, beautiful, had put on some weight,
and we hugged and she apologised for her 'problem with cakes'
before I'd said even the slightest word of encouragement to
her... We escaped the wake and crawled into this abandoned
bookshop somewhere down a dense cobbled street. Lots of
the shelves were just filled with my books; they were directly
my own shelves. The first thing I picked up was a tattered
pamphlet that was falling apart. It was by another ??? and it
was published in 1985 which was probably before their birth,
but we were so entranced by it. When you turned the pages it
played classic Windows XP sounds, and there were dolphins
on the cover. I didn't even get to the poems; it was such a cool
publication to just look at, cooing. There were treasure pools
of change inside it, so I lifted a defunct pound coin to put in

the jar to pay for the book. The crazy anachronism archive, how is that. I was so excited to message ??? and tell them what we'd found, but I also didn't want to go back and the imperative to go back was like someone telling me to wake up out of the dream, wash my hands, and I was so desperate to stay curled up in that bookshop. Aimless, blurring. To become their resident feline, learning to read all over as fate touched me gently behind the ears. It was a kind of fame.

Not sure

Unwanted milk,
always so desperate.

Oh, *hey there*, I'm that tattered
barista, inside a kind
of puffy dream,
reading encouragement in all this spilling.

Check me out, mopping up all slightest starts
or searching for action in abandoned pools.

To learn to read over,
this failure at falling,
this rushing at telling,
this witness of machine.

Not sure how it happened, but
I am actually living inside a Windows XP,
Glasgow, all gorgeous in here.

The city tugs at my watery words, before
the sleep falls apart.

Is this a kind of fame?

Somniloquy: A Little Kilo of Dreams

Here we present you a bundle of our dreams, wrapped in something like a rhythm, or did we mean a ribbon? '*More or less*', Hélène Cixous writes in *Dream I Tell You* (2003): '*A big book or a little kilo of dreams. Consider the weight of each dream; or of a thought; or of a kiss*'. The dream is a nip, it says *You're here. I'm here*. It's delicious, bright red of any chord, cord. Why do we write this.

There was a time, May 2018, that an accident happened, in response to a trauma. We found ourselves at a loss for what to say, sipping gin in the bar with a hug in its name. So I said, Kirsty said, let's share our dreams. And I said, Maria said, I've already started. A dream is a portion of what you can't say, excepting. All summer, we wrote dreams because we weren't writing poems, or the poems weren't writing themselves exactly. Instead, we were writing fiction: [*inside the box*] *a collection* (Kirsty), *The Indigo Hours* (Maria). Little twin novellas. Something was coming to fruition & the dreams kept coming, or at least almost.

We were not reading Freud, but we were concerned with icebergs. An obsession developed with that point upon waking, everything melting, and only in that liminal hour of the Google Doc would it crystallise. We sucked upon those little scoops of sleep before they escaped through other streams of thought. The dream ledger was a record of what was left out in daily life, what bubbled up or froze in a space that could not sound itself out. We did not speak irl of our dreams, but we sent each other messages. Then, there was a party, Maria's birthday, where we read aloud our dreams to the folks of Shakespeare Street. The dreams made us drunker, the drunkenness itself became a theory of dreams. *I love you*, we'd shout to the blinking white of a morning page. Here was teenage neon, eked to the dark. It turned us inverse, to excess. It was the glittering trash-pile we wrote from later.

Kirsty had a dream that was more like an essay. So the dream itself was an essay and you had to enter the essay to follow the dream. There was a kind of paragraph additive, chemical almost, you could call it a pulse: 'a friend at a sleepover [...] comparing dreams to merry-go-rounds. You hop on for several rides; you remember the dream. You get too dizzy and stagger away; you have dreamt but you refuse to remember'. This dream occurred in early June, the roses were heady as fairground lights and candyfloss sweet. The dreams became layers, petals you could peel from a whorl and make into index. Who was this you. In the dreams we were always speaking to someone, if not each other. Occasionally we forgot who wrote what, the voices wove around each other, knitting strange colours and shapes into a tapestry that almost made an image. Some dreams were wiggling lines. Some dreams would not stop spiralling. You cannot always shout stop to a dream. You fall back. A dream into a dream into a dream.

And then she woke up and it was all a dream. When people asked what we were working on, there was always this pause. Were these dreams or fictions? How much did we make up in a state of amnesia, did it matter? We felt dream-writing was denigrated, 'feminised', considered cliché; we found in dream-writing the story of a play that was serious, recuperative, generous. Is story itself a non-dream, and what dream plasma was charged or erased by our narrative imposition? We tried mostly to listen, wedded to Cixous' idea of dream 'intemporality': the time lived in dream as a bubble, an ageless space. When we dream it's like we die every night. And to wake is to feel something burst inside you, a smouldering tone that lingers, whispers, *yes here*. It takes writing to know this, setting aside the variant weight of each dream, like a death. The longer we wrote through the summer, the heavier the dreams got, as though water-logged from a current whose flow was a latent release, a lag in tempo. The longer we wrote through the summer, the lighter we felt in ourselves. The dreams came out of us more easily: they said, *find me. I am your insistent inner child.*

Sometimes, we mixed up the dream and the real, a confusion of flavours. I would be like, what happened last night? I would be like, was it me or you? Sugar or salt? Our realities would shimmer awhile beside each other. The magic of coincidence would happen: one night we each met our favourite celebrities. Dreams became the porous cumulus of a mutual thought. At times, narratives would meet and then separate, thin and stretch and often clot. Dreams as little deaths, humours, failings, stains, layers of sheets; dreams as gestures towards a world that was filtered with future inclinations. Dreams escaping fatalism, making the cleaves that would open time in streams and streams.

So we would talk in our typing. Could we call the dream book a kind of commons? There was such a confusion of scale: the micro and the macro would converge and drown inside each other. A season passed in four phases of sleep; the year quartered itself into summer. What experience we shared of real life would diverge in our dreams. Kirsty and Maria lived ambiently within Kirsty-Maria's cloud storage. Intoxicating effect: the dream as *pharmakon*, both poison and cure for the lack that gave the project its birth. A way to be inside and out, both inside the body and looking back, analysing at the same time we messed up in our sense of a *happening*. This reality, indifferent to questions of style or quality, felt 'real' by fact of its infinite turn.

To write our dreams was a calling back, a calling forward. These dreams reflect the rose-headed whorl of a summer, petalling and shedding: presence, return, beauty, connection, pleasure, colour, sound and shame. We had to pluck but a few from the ledger to make a slender book; the rest of the dreams would melt on a server somewhere, alive in their absence and presence. We collect the silliest, most beautiful dreams. The ribbon of the bundle would run in a mobius form, the reader (this tender *you*, hello) would look for a surface, a face to surf. We dream and untie ourselves, nightly.

*

This essay is taken from a longer collaborative work: Soft Friction.

Contributors

Saskia McCracken and **Greg Thomas** are Glasgow-based writers and editors. Greg's publications include *Cloud Cover* (Essence Press 2018) and *Border Blurs: Concrete Poetry in England and Scotland* (Liverpool University Press 2019) and Saskia's include *Imperative Utopia* (-algia press 2021). Their poem draws on the South Glasgow Heritage and Environment Trust archives.

Maria Sledmere is editor-in-chief at SPAM Press and a member of A+E Collective. Publications include *nature sounds without nature sounds* (Sad Press), *Rainbow Arcadia* (Face Press), *Chlorophyllia* (orangeapplepress) and *neutral milky halo* (Guillemot Press). With Rhian Williams, she co-edited *the weird folds: everyday poems from the anthropocene* (Dostoyevsky Wannabe).

Kirsty Dunlop lives in Glasgow and writes poems, short stories, electronic literature and collaborative work. She is a DFA candidate in Creative Writing at the University of Glasgow and is the poetry and nonfiction editor at SPAM Press. Recent work includes a broadside collaboration with nicky melville, THE FACT THAT, out with GONG FARM.

Agata Maslowska was born in Poland and lives in Scotland. Her poetry and fiction have appeared in *Edinburgh Review, New Writing Scotland, Scottish PEN's New Writing,* and *Gutter Maga-*

zine, among others. She is the recipient of the Hawthornden Writing Fellowship and the Gillian Purvis Award for New Writing. Twitter @AgataMaslowska

Sam Healy is an Edinburgh-based musician and the main vocalist and songwriter of the band North Atlantic Oscillation. He has also released solo albums under Sand. He is a member of Ray Interactive, art and design studio specialising in interactive technologies, creative coding and generative graphics.

Denise Bonetti is a Capricorn, and the Managing Editor of the post-internet poetry magazine & press SPAM. She is the author of 20 Pack, published by If A Leaf Falls Press, and Probs Too Late For a Snog Now :'(((, published with SPAM Press. She lives in London.

Tessa Berring and **Kathrine Sowerby** are poet/artists who live in Edinburgh and Glasgow respectively. They write, make books, and perform collaboratively as Usual Shoe and their work can be found in DATABLEED, Blackbox Manifold, 3AM Magazine, ZARF, A) GLIMPSE) OF) and Tentacular.

Nia Benchimol and **Rhian Williams** are writers based in Glasgow, near the River Kelvin. Rhian recently co-edited, *the weird folds: everyday poems from the anthropocene* with Maria Sledmere (Dostoyevsky Wannabe, 2020). Nia has been exploring different ways of writing and thinking about the non-human world, especially birds and dogs. Rhian writes and reviews poetry and film for Spam Press and MAP magazine.

Georgi Gill is an Edinburgh-based writer and PhD researcher at the University of Edinburgh. Her poems explore themes including the personal and cultural impact of illness and queer history. Georgi's work has been widely published and her first collection, *Limbo* is forthcoming with Blue Diode Press in October 2021.

Gillian Shirreffs has a Doctor of Fine Arts degree in Creative Writing. Her fiction explores the world of illness and her narrative nonfiction interrogates medical objects, places, and spaces. Her work has appeared in The Interpreter's House, thi wurd magazine, *Tales from a Cancelled Country*, and The Polyphony, amongst others.

K Patrick and **Adrien Howard** are writers and artists both based in Glasgow. They have been collaborating since 2019 and work across experimental narrative, prose, poetry and publication making. Writing from a place of friendship, they form narratives which explore their relationships to place, time, memory and transgender existence.

T. Person is a writer and editor living in Glasgow. Their most recent pamphlet, *Decalcomania*, was published by —algia and they co-edit orangeapplepress. Poems and works have been included in Gutter magazine, Trickhouse press, Radiophrenia, and Erotoplasty. They currently writing a long poem centred around the queue for a club.

Gaar Adams is a writer and doctoral candidate at the University of Glasgow. His work has appeared in *The Atlantic, Foreign Policy, Rolling Stone, Al Jazeera, Slate, VICE* and more. He is a London Library Emerging Writer and is writing a book on queerness and migration in the Middle East.

EC Lewis is a Glasgow based poet and writer. Their poetry has appeared in several publications including *Southchild Lit, -algia, Fairy Piece MAG*! Their writing engages with the minutiae of life, examining the ordinary in order to further explore the beauty in what it means to be human.

Kiah Endelman Music is an artist and writer based in Glasgow. Her work has been featured in *MAP Magazine* and *PUB Journal*, performed at The Glasgow Women's Library and The Deptford Project and exhibited at Govan Project Space. She is also an associate editor of *NOTHING PERSONAL* magazine.

Gwen Dupré is from Dumfries & Galloway and lives in Glasgow. Her writing has appeared in *MAP Magazine, Lucy Writers* and *Noesis. The Moon City*, a curatorial project, was shown at Govan Project Space in 2020. She is currently working on the philosophy of Simone Weil.

Esther Draycott is a writer and PhD candidate based between the University of Glasgow and Glasgow School of Art. Her thesis is on a performative history of style in postindustrial

Glasgow. She is an associate editor of NOTHING PERSONAL magazine.

Fionn Duffy & **Eilidh Nuala Duffy** grew up together in Glasgow. Fionn lives there now and Eilidh is quite far away. Eilidh is a writer, Fionn is an artist; both work in their own way with other people to make things.

Juana Adcock is a poet and translator. She has published *Manca* (Argonautica, 2019), which explores the anatomy of violence in the Mexican drug war, and *Split* (Blue Diode Press, 2019) which was a Poetry Book Society Choice and was included in the Guardian's Best Poetry of 2019.

Shehzar Doja is Founder/Editor-in-Chief of The Luxembourg Review and Poetry Reviews Editor at Gutter. His poetry and translations have appeared in *New Welsh Review, Pratik, Modern Poetry in Translation, Voice and Verses, Ceremony, Smoke, Poems from the Edge of Extinction, The Centenary Collection for Edwin Morgan, Fundstücke-Trouvailles* and more.

Jim Colquhoun and **Jamie McNeill** are artists and writers from the Lands of Nether Pollok in the Barony of Mearns. They both lay claim to descent from the denizens of the lost hamlet of Pooktoun.

Jamie Bolland is a teacher, skateboarder, and artist working with writing and performance (www.slomo.scot).

Mark Briggs is an artist, writer and filmmaker based in Glasgow. Currently working out of Tramway he has exhibited both nationally and internationally independently and under the guise of gastower.com.

Rosie Roberts is an artist, writer and filmmaker based in Glasgow. Her research surrounds the poetic haptics of everyday occurrence, documentary, speculative writings and relevance/commons/locality.

Lucy Cash and **Luke Pell** carry out writing through an embodied, practice-based enquiry. Of late we've been immersed in thinking deeply & lightly; with caring harder, & with quiet queerings. Working across form, we have been making presenting and performing a practice concerned with the choreographic, for a double of decades. *but felt for, back & forth* is haunted by some of the after-glow of words by Italo Calvino; Luce Irigaray; Ocean Vuong and Peter Gizzi, as well as our own intimate experiences in the performance worlds of Nigel Charnock; Adrian Howells; Anna Krzystek and Janice Parker.

Anjeli Caderamanpulle is a poet living in Glasgow. She is a St.Mungo's Mirrorball Clydebuilt apprentice for 2021 and recipient of a second life grant from the Edwin Morgan Trust. Her pamphlet Boys was published by SPAM Press in 2020. She edits Meet Cute Zine and her poetry has been published in Gutter and Adjacent Pineapple.

Joanne Lee is an artist who lives and works in Glasgow. Lee graduated from Sculpture and Environmental Art at Glasgow School of Art 2019. Their practice is interested in interrogating what it means to make and see from the periphery. Approaching making as a way of translating the subjective experience of being in the world and making space for new narratives centred in embodied knowledge through moving image, text and installation.

Jane Goldman lives in Edinburgh and is Reader in English at the University of Glasgow. She likes anything a word can do. Her poems have appeared in a number of magazines and anthologies including *Gutter, SPAM, Zarf, Blackbox Manifold,* and *Adjacent Pineapple*, as well as in *the weird folds: every- day poems from the Anthropocene*, edited by Maria Sledmere and Rhian Williams (Dostoyevsky Wannabe, 2020), and in the pamphlet, *Border Thoughts* (Sufficient Place/Leamington Books, 2014). *SEKXPHRASTIKS* (Dostoyevsky Wannabe, 2021) is her first full length collection.

Matthew Kinlin lives and writes in Glasgow. His novels Teenage Hallucination (Orbis Tertius Press) and Curse Red, Curse Blue, Curse Green (Sweat Drenched Press) were released in 2021

Loll Jung is a human animal usually found residing in Glasgow, Scotland, with poetic, essayistic, and critical work published by Nothing Personal, SPAM, Adjacent Pineapple, Gutter, MAP, and BlueHouse. Their current research interests lie in examining geological and human processes of decline through hybrid essaying and poetry, and grappling with intersections between mythology, ecology, and memory.

Tim Knights is a filmmaker and writer based in Glasgow. His work has screened at festivals and venues like Sheffield Doc:Fest, SQIFF, the BFI and the V&A Dundee.

Christopher Owen is an artist. He also co-curated 'The Man with Night Sweats' (Kingsgate Studios 2017). Owen lives in Glasgow.

Printed in Great Britain
by Amazon

77921277R00237